U0076380

小樹系列

Little Trees

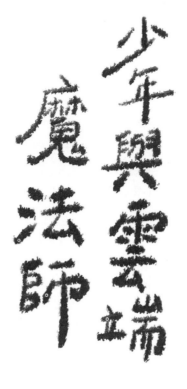

少年與雲端魔法師

The Boy and the Cloud Magician

推薦序
陪伴少年的指引

陳宏義（法務部矯正署誠正中學校長）

　　感恩有機會拜讀幸惠、律君師姊陪伴少年歷程的大作，勾起我與少年的初次接觸感受，如同是生活在兩個平行時空，或者是感覺這青少年來自外太空。在矯正學校與少年的互動中，了解到學生因各項情緒衝動下的非行行為及其後果，往往與書中描繪有相呼應處。

　　矯正學校，讓我們有機會與受感化教育的孩子接觸，慶幸能陪伴他們走過這一段青澀歲月。透過書中第一個描述到的「自信心」主題，讓我想起學生週記裡的一段話：我們已經和失敗熟得不能再熟了，從今以後我想換個朋友交交看，和成功打打交道……。孩子的企圖從過往的「什麼都不能做、什麼都做不好」的印象中走出來，很高興我們能提供平台，讓孩子開展各種的可能性！

　　本書有一套完整對於孩子陪伴的引導歷程：從安全感建立、青少年的人際關係、憤怒情緒的控制、面對挫折的學習、建立良好勤奮習性、親子關係與感恩的心、金錢運用與助人的快樂、對失落親情的修復以及最後離別議題的處理等等。透過故事的進行，可以讓我們對於引導陪伴有充分理解。並將之對應在矯正學校陪伴孩子的歷程中。這些故事參照和閱讀經驗，能給予從事少年陪伴工作者重要啟發：與孩子站在一起，共同陪伴孩子成長，運用科技新知，引導學習與創新體驗，將開拓孩子未來無限的可能！

感佩幸惠、律君師姊將陪伴少年成長的歷程化為文字故事，引領我們循序有方地陪伴所有孩子——無論是順利長成或曾經迷惘者。很榮幸受邀先睹為快，鄭重推薦給家有青少年的父母親及陪伴少年的所有人。

雲端庫存的七把鑰匙

林幸惠

　　您看到了嗎？遠方的雲端，偶爾會閃耀著光輝，那是魔法師藏在後方，正在管理著雲端的庫存，那裡保存著有形或無形的過去、現在與未來幻想的資料──還有您每天不知不覺累積的資料！

　　故事，是這樣開始的……

　　有一天，魔法師忽然莫名地跌落人間，巧遇沮喪的少年，魔法師利用庫存的資料幫助少年走過徬徨的時刻。

　　雲端庫存的資料，可以涵蓋天地包羅萬象，尤其是家族的系統。而這個系列故事的發想，即源自「家庭系統排列」的核心內涵，家庭系統排列是心理治療領域的一環，是德國心理學家伯特・海寧格（Bert Hellinger）所開發出來的，用於家庭治療，與傳遞許多家族情緒及未竟之事的信息，讓後來的世代，可以洞察家族的深層心理狀態與行動分析，進而彌補缺憾。

　　本書以魔法師的資料為經，少年的生活故事為緯，策略性引導少年建立信心、學習溝通、和解與看見愛，進而改善親子關係，並開發社會情懷，這就是家庭和諧的關係法則，也是支持生命成長的動力。故事中魔法師的角色，是由年輕的 Kelly 所創意發想；而賦予故事少年靈動活現的對話與行為者，則來自本書共同作者律君日常與孩子們互動的經歷。故事文字採中英對照，期以簡潔文字，讓父母與小孩都易閱讀，親近國際語言，進而開拓視野。有趣回甘的故事，不僅能滋養自己，更是豐富的成長資源。

故事中藏有七把鑰匙，如同谷歌的搜尋引擎，都可以萃取出每把鑰匙的行動密碼，被霸凌時、沒信心時、無法專心讀書時，怎麼辦？如何與朋友相處，如何與大人溝通，如何處理情緒，還有感恩與原諒過去。每一把雖然都以感恩為基點，利他為通關密碼，但最有趣的是少年的對話串起本書的笑點，頗能令人感同身受。

家長們可以笑看本書，回憶青春時期的年少輕狂，進而能尊重與理解孩子的反抗情緒。少年們可以透過本書，當遇到類似事件，可以同理彼此，就不會感到沮喪、孤單、脆弱無助，而是學會排除疑惑、重拾面對現實的勇氣。不同年齡層的讀者，倘若遇到這些問題時，也可以從中找到支撐自己的各種方式，並發展出不一樣的人生觀。其實，宇宙人生的道理都在庫存裡，也就是在人的本性裡。。

記得小時候，生病躺在床上，讓棉被層層地包裹，如同被許多愛呵護著。仰望著有鏽染紋的牆壁，沿著紋路幻想故事，遐想著鄰居孩子們，嘻笑歡樂地穿梭在田野中，還聽得到鳥鳴蟲叫，説起來有點好笑，但在想像力無垠馳騁中，我愉快地過了病痛這一關，而那段時光，也成為珍藏我心底的記憶。隨著年紀漸長當了志工，有因緣去監獄採訪受刑人時，才深深警覺到，世上有許多命運坎坷，連幻想的力量都被摧毀的孩子，他們只剩下陰影，經歷了許多慘事而孤立無援，或長期被傷痛囚困著，因此有著層層疊疊的關卡需要跨越。他們的生命需要被重新轉化，信心需要被鼓勵，自卑感更需要被補償。因此萌生了出版本書的念頭，希望能喚起大家來支持他們，讓他們相信人間有愛。

地球依然轉個不停，少年的你，可以帶著父親的祝福，母親的關懷，勇敢地邁向人生的目標、道途的遠方。

作者序
找到志同道合的人生戰友
陳律君

這本書產生於聽幸惠師姊說了許多少年的故事之後。

在聽完故事以後，我想以重新檢視的方式，和少年討論過往人際對待上到底哪裡出問題，才導致了目前的窘境。沒有人不想把事情閃亮亮地完成，但又總是事與願違，關鍵到底哪裡出錯了呢？

必須找出問題點！不然沒完沒了……

在書裡，也會看到很多眼熟的經常聽到的家庭對話，其實大家都活在既有的行為模式裡，說的話一樣，選的早餐店也一樣，上學的路線一樣，所以犯的錯也都一樣，但真的都一樣嗎？怎樣才會不一樣？怎樣才不會再開始另一個討人厭的循環？

我小時候看過一部電影《駭客任務》（*The Matrix*），講有一群「覺醒的人類」離開了既定模式存活在程式之外，最大的目的是讓所有被慣性模式控制的人類從程式中解脫。我在電影裡學到了覺醒的重要性。當然，也是有人很願意活在慣性中，這也沒什麼對錯，問題在於是被迫？還是自願？這本書裡有一點這方面的蛛絲馬跡哦。

書中主人翁專門是為來自不完整原生家庭的人類設計

的。不完整原生家庭，常因牽絆於現實生活的各種困難，導致家庭成員產生情緒問題，並在相互反應下出現心結、人格不健全諸問題，最終，他們可能總在社會上找補自己缺失的那塊——作者們稱之為「心靈密碼」。但這些事學校並沒有教，如果自己又沒有找到對的方法應對，那壞的結果就會像滾雪球般一發不可收拾，然後就……你懂的……一直囧（窘）下去！

這個時候，如果那位主人翁剛好是你，有多少次會在心裡吶喊：「誰來幫幫我！？」

書裡的少年知道自己不夠好，但又不知如何才能改變，矛盾是他的本色，掙扎是出於本能，因此經常到處碰壁。但別說是他，作者我也是如此，而且我後來發現，身邊好多朋友也一樣。

在寫故事的同時，我經常反思，只有這些少年才有這種被錯待的心境嗎？大人不都經常說他們也都是這麼長大的嗎？那應該也有許多人在成長過程中有相同的挫折吧。只是長大了，以為事情小了；久了，就沒有關係了；但，其實不是哦。

心理治療有一個學派，以「家族治療」幫助人們找尋各自的密碼來補齊心理的缺憾，幫助人們重建人格，重啟自信，重塑價值。家族治療絕對不是萬靈丹，也不是作者的寥寥數語就能全部概括，但它確實是許多心理問題的良方。經由本書另一作者的闡述，我了解到家族治療的方法及效用，發現其中的心理觀察角度好有趣，於是想用這個方法一起寫一本書給大家。或許看完這本書後，大家可以一起來了解為什麼有「家族治療」這個學派。心理學，真的很好玩。

本書，是有關於「改變」的小說。

我深深以為，不僅是青少年，我們大人其實也超多問題的，所以我們對待別人的方式也不盡然全對，不盡然不能被檢討，要相信，世界上沒有完美的人。希望大家能做到的不是相互指責不完美，而是互相補足彼此的缺陷。

這世界不是伊甸園，我們不可能離群索居，所以就一定會存在人際關係。在人類社會裡，家庭系統中，難道只有這些我們以為的「問題人」才有問題？有沒有可能，少年們的爸媽在小時候也有過成長挫折，導致他們有一部分「沒長好」，才會用「不酷的方式」對待自己的小孩？

寫作本書，並非要透過文字讓讀者知書達理，也不是在避免我的青少年讀者們誤入歧途，只是想告訴大家──「人生，就是一場戰鬥！」要打得漂亮，就要經常改變戰術。作者也還在努力戰鬥，每一個人都是，無論老少，你並不孤單。

改變，一直都是人生的最大課題，而那個主導權，在你心上。

讀到這裡，你可能不見得覺得自己需要改變，但事實是你已經回不去了！

contents

目錄

第一章
CHAPTER 1

你從哪裡來？
Where Are You From?

It was a beautiful sunny afternoon. Lush trees, flowers, and grass blanketed a glittering, dreamlike riverbank. Dressed in a rainbow outfit and holding a tablet computer in one hand, "Data" was admiring the beauty of nature. "This is what one might call a paradise. Breezes, the sun, the grass—so much better than the digital world and the Cloud. I don't understand why humans love hoarding things, whether in real life or in the Cloud," said Data. All of a sudden, he felt a pebble flying and hitting his shoes as he heard a loud cursing shriek, "Who cares about anybody? I sure don't, and neither does anybody else in the world." With each curse, the boy threw out another pebble, farther and more forceful than the last one.

Data looked in the direction of where the pebbles had come from. A boy, full of rage with more pebbles in his hand, was about to throw the next one out. He stepped in front of the boy, raised his hand to stop him, and calmly asked the boy, "You seem frustrated, but I don't quite understand the logic of how throwing pebbles randomly towards a stranger will help you vent your frustration."

He scratched and tilted his head a couple of times before continuing in a pensive tone, "Well, I'm not particularly good at comprehending human emotions. Why do humans cry or

風和日麗的下午，河堤邊的河水清淨，樹叢枝葉茂盛，小花小草像在編織著美夢，「庫哥」穿著散發光譜的衣服，拿著平板，喃喃自語著：「哎呀～有風、有陽光、有小草，這才是真正天堂，比雲端好太多了，人類特別愛囤積物質，連在雲端也要囤積一堆有的沒的，真是不好說。」庫哥躺在下坡草地上無奈地自言自語，在灌木叢遮蔽下，微笑地望著河面，正享受著大自然陽光空氣水的滋潤，靜得透明的時光。突然，他的鞋子，被石頭砸中了，還聽到咒罵加哭聲：

　　「都不要過來啊，就都不要找我！找不到算了！我也不稀罕你們！誰要管你們！誰要你們管！」每唸一句還丟一顆石頭，越丟越用力，越丟越遠。

　　正想一探究竟誰亂丟的石頭，卻看到一個少年正氣呼呼地進行自我放棄模式，庫哥便喊：「哇哩咧，你這哪來不好說的渾小子，怨氣沖天，碎碎唸又亂丟石頭還丟那麼用力，都丟到我身上了！」庫哥站起來走出灌木叢向少年走去。

　　「你要不就告訴我怎麼了，要不我也學你丟你石頭。」庫哥逗他說：「不過我不會學你哭哦，太腦包了，

laugh on a whim?"

For a moment, the boy thought that he was in trouble for hitting the guy, so he was trying to weasel his way out with a half-hearted apology. However, just one look at the guy was enough to stop the boy in his tracks. The "person" was shiny, wearing a bodysuit of rainbow colors and, oh man, his face! He had wide yet slanted, bluish brown eyes that covered almost half of his face. He also had a sharp but small and narrow nose that could be a coat hanger. Strangely he had a full head of blackish blond hair which doesn't really go with the rest of his physique, and his translucent skin tone made him almost transparent. The boy gasped, "Are you…. are you, um, normal?"

Data stared back at the boy. "My looks aren't organically grown. They are coded. If you'd like, I can make myself look like a Martian on another day, but right now I haven't taken your preference into consideration."

Data was pleased with the repartee he was having with a human, and he was also rather impressed by his own sense of humor and quick wit that computer algorithms had directed him to manifest.

"What gobbledygook are you talking about? What code?

呵呵，我實在是不懂你們人類為什麼那麼愛哭愛笑。」

少年以為自己砸到人了，想隨便撇一句「對不起」就逃跑，趕緊瞄了一眼面前的「人」，瞄完一楞，完全可以看出被忽然出現的「人」嚇傻了：「你……」他仔細看了一下庫哥瞪大了眼，遲疑地開口：「你……長壞了嗎？」少年見對方的臉既東方也洋氣，像混血兒，可是眼睛大得有點印度血統，鼻樑不挺也不塌，頭髮倒是黑的，膚色說不出來是黃還是白，還是有點棕？最主要是他覺得眼前這個「人」整個顏色有點淡，淡到快成透明了。

庫哥頓了頓，說：「這不是用長的，這是編碼編出來的，如果你喜歡，我改天編個火星人給你？不過我目前沒想考慮你的喜歡。」庫哥心情好地和少年抬槓，他也是第一次真實與人類對話，感覺自己在幽默感和臨場反應運算能力還是頗優。

少年說：「在說什麼鬼，什麼編碼？什麼火星人？」他忽然領悟，說出了心裡的猜想：「你不是人？！」

What Martian?" Then it dawned on the boy. "You're not human?" the boy blurted out his suspicion.

Data's head suddenly made a 360-degree horizontal rotation as if to applaud the boy's newfound insight. Aghast, the boy muttered, "What are you, then? A ghost? No it's bright daylight, so you can't be that. Are you a figment of my imagination? No, your image just seems too real to be in my imagination. Ah, you are an alien! Aren't you here to abduct me?"

Data was bemused by the boy's varied reactions from being incredulous and agitated to being frightened. He countered, "What do you have that's going to be worth my trouble abducting you, bro?"

Data's question crushed the boy. "Yep, you're right. I am completely useless and worthless. You won't wring anything valuable out of me. Mr. Alien, you're better off abducting somebody else," the boy said.

The boy was convinced that someone as worthless as he would not even deserve the honor of an extraterrestrial abduction.

Data didn't understand what had caused the boy's melancholy reaction to the conversation. Was it because the

庫哥的頭瞬間水平轉了 360 度，一副「你現在才知道」的表情看著少年。少年又驚又楞，一會兒後才出聲：「那你是什麼？鬼嗎？現在是白天，應該不是……你怎麼出現的？你怎麼會在這裡？你來幹嘛？還是你只是我的幻想？難不成你是要綁架我的外星人？！」

　　庫哥看著少年時而懷疑地皺眉，時而激動地驚恐，時而又像是自言自語的表情，都不知道怎麼對他了，直到少年說他是來綁架自己的外星人時，他笑了：「你得要有什麼可以讓我綁走的利用價值啊，老兄。」

　　少年一聽，臉色瞬間垮了下來，慢慢低下頭說：「也對，我沒什麼用，你抓了我就算用榨汁機把我榨乾也擠不出一丁點殘渣。我看你還是去抓別人吧……」少年覺得被外星人綁架這種高級奇遇，應該不會發生在他這種可有可無、連自己都不知道有什麼自我價值的人身上。

　　庫哥一聽，以為自己說了什麼傷人的話，看來幽默感和臨場反應運算程式還是該修改一下，於是進入彌

algorithm for his humor and his human interactions was not quite as mature as he anticipated? In this situation, a good model would call for a corrective action. He said to the boy, "I'm sorry, I don't know you well enough to say anything about your worth. Please do not feel bad about whatever I just said."

He reached his hand into the deep front pocket of his rainbow jacket as if fishing for something and said to the boy, "To show my sincerity, let me simulate this conversation on my super tablet, and I will come up with a better response. Give me a minute."

The boy, still self-pitying, didn't understand much of what the alien had said. The boy wasn't really listening anyway, but he couldn't take his eyes off the flat, shining thing in the alien's hands, which, for the moment, made him forget all his woes that had led to his melancholy.

"What's that?" The boy was stunned for the third time today, overwhelmed by all the new encounters, not least the futuristic tablet that seemed a gazillion generations ahead of his time. He wondered if his own brain would be spacious enough to house extraterrestrial lives (or non-lives) and the next big thing that might come along. It appeared that his brain would surely run out of space.

Data explained patiently again.

"As I told you before, I've used this super tablet to model human behavior and run scenarios. It has a quantum computer powered by a multi-dimensional neural network that rivals the complexity of human brains but processes infinitely faster. In plain language, it's a high fidelity computer learning model of human interaction on a chip."

"You've overestimated me. Do you really think I'd get all that?" The boy said and gave a polite yet awkward smile.

His attempt to explain in vain, Data just knew that a human mind is rather limited in comprehending his existence. Without wasting another minute, he said to the boy, "Let's play a little game on my tablet."

He walked with the tablet over to the boy and twisted two fingers, a shiny bright curve floated in midair above the tablet.

"This curve represents your life's trajectory. Everyone has a curve like this. Everything that has happened in your life so far is plotted on this curve, which gets longer with age until you die."

Data picked out a small dot on the curve and zoomed in with his fingers as light danced on the screen to form a 3D hologram of a place.

庫哥再次耐心解釋：「剛剛不是説了嗎，超模平板，是種以異次元類人腦模式智慧為運算主幹的集合型超模擬體平板，以你可以理解的方式，就是可以溝通和感知人類意識和情感的平板電腦。」

　　少年：「你太高估我了，你以為這樣説我就懂了嗎。」少年給了庫哥一個尷尬又不失禮貌的微笑。

　　庫哥徒勞了一場，但他早知道人類沒辦法理解他的存在，於是也不再解釋，直接對少年説：「我用我的平板跟你玩個小遊戲。」庫哥拿著平板靠近少年，平板經過兩瞬的運轉後浮出一條光軸，庫哥向少年解釋：「這條光軸是你的生命軌跡，每個人都會有一條，在你身上發生了什麼都會一點一點地增添在這上面，越來越長，直到死亡。」

　　緊接庫哥就用兩根手指頭捏出一段再放大，平板又發出幾道光形成一個模擬 3D 投影在平板上。

That place was the boy's classroom. He saw his rowdy classmates, the usual gang, laughing and monkeying around, but his seat was empty. The assistant class leader walked by his empty seat and asked, "Is Wendi not here today? Does anybody know why?"

One of the kids who was laughing and chatting the loudest retorted, "Haven't seen him yet. Maybe he's gone mad again?"

All the kids roared with laughter, to which the assistant class leader replied with good humor, "Next time when you're absent, I'll mark that you've gone mad, too."

The whole class was now laughing out of control, except the rowdy ones who shot the rest of the class dirty looks.

The boy became quite annoyed with what he was watching. Calmly, Data said again, "The show is far from over. Just sit tight and watch till the end."

One of the kids sitting a few rows diagonally behind the empty seat spoke up. "He's been pretty absent-minded on most days at school, and he wouldn't even chat with us during recess or after school. I have no idea what's on his mind. You think he might have ditched school today?"

Data turned to look at Wendi and said, "You said you had no friends? Even when you don't think anybody is looking,

少年看到影像出現自己班上的狀況，同學們嬉鬧著，自己的座位空著。特別騷動的還是那幾位，副班長走過空座位旁，問了問附近的同學：「游文諦今天沒來嗎？有誰知道為什麼嗎？」

　　嬉鬧的其中一位回了話：「誰知道他為什麼沒來，可能又發神經了吧。」

　　幾個同學隨著他大笑了幾聲，副班長倒是很幽默回了那位同學：「下次你沒來我就知道你也是發神經了，對吧？」換其他同學大笑了，不過招來那嬉鬧的幾個同學瞪視。

　　少年看到這裡心情更不好了，庫哥不疾不徐的聲音傳了過來：

　　「戲還沒演完，要看到最後。」

　　空位子斜後方座位上的同學說話了：「我看他每天上學都無精打采的，下課也不跟我們說話，不知道他在想什麼。他會不會今天翹課了？」

　　這時庫哥側頭看了少年一眼說：「怎麼沒朋友，你看，你同學也是默默在觀察你，每個朋友都是先從觀察開始建立起友誼，你老看著自己，等著別人來理你，結

there are always people watching you. Friendship starts with taking an interest in other people instead of focusing only on yourself and waiting for others to take an interest in you. You don't even know who your classmates are, but some of them actually know you. Open your eyes and look around. You want friends? These are people who are very likely going to be your buddies in the future."

Upon hearing this, there was a twinkle of light in the boy's eye that seemed to indicate a deepened understanding, but the light slowly faded away.

Data ventured, "Are you shy?" Wendi took a furtive glance at him as if to say, "None of your business." However, he blushed, belying his true emotion. Data could not understand, and muttered indignantly, "Man! None of my business? If it were not for me, you wouldn't even knowwhat a supercomputer looks like and what your classmates say about you behind your back. This is like a gift from heaven, yet you don't seem to appreciate it. Your chances of meeting me are actually less than your chances of hitting the jackpot." He continued, "Yeah, this is kind of weird. How was it that I ran into you on my trip out of the Cloud?"

No sooner had he finished that thought than his eyes

果你連了解自己的同學都還沒做好，同學已經先觀察過你了，張大眼睛，看看別人。你想要朋友？這些都是未來的哥們啊！」

少年眼中閃爍著不可思議，卻也好似懂了什麼一樣，但剛剛才亮起的眼神又慢慢趨向黯然。

庫哥一看猜想道：「會不好意思啊？」

少年又斜看了他一眼，擺明了在說「要你管」，臉上跟著不小心泛了一絲絲害羞的紅。

「呵！還嫌我狗拿耗子？如果我不那麼雞婆，你會有機會看到我的超模？有機會看到你同學在你背後的反應？天上掉下來的禮物你不要，這機率我看比中大樂透頭獎還來得低很多。」庫哥見少年不識貨的表情實在氣不過，也把他看得太扁了吧。

庫哥又自言自語起來：「對耶，說也奇怪，我從雲端下來，為什麼偏偏碰到你？」

說完，這兩個人立刻四目對視，不過沒迸出什麼電光火花，只冒出了一堆問號。

met the boy's eyes, which ignited no sparks but only endless question marks.

The boy, on the other hand, also wondered why he had been talking to a strange extraterrestrial for as long as he had. All the cautions one would normally exercise toward a stranger had been thrown out of the window. Was it because "he" was not a real person or because his gadgets were just too cool to resist? Anyway, the boy was very curious about Data.

The boy, wanting to test him, said, "So, how can I start making friends?"

Data answered with a counter-question, "First, ask yourself why you need friends. What can you do with friends?"

"Well, so I have somebody to talk to. Nobody in my class wants to talk to me. They taunt me instead."

"Okay. Is that all? You just want someone who will listen to you? That's easy."

Data waved his five fingers counterclockwise at the 3D image and produced a holographic scene where a student was squatting in front of a school garden. The boy recognized the student right away.

"That's Gao Haoping! He hates going to school, too. The teacher often made us stand in class in time-outs. What's he

少年心裡想著，自己是怎麼跟一個陌生「人」聊起來的，莫名其妙的不排斥，會不會是因為「他」不是真的人，或許是因為他的「裝備優勢」完全吸引了自己，反正少年對庫哥充滿了好奇。

　　於是故意試探庫哥的能耐，問道：「那我怎樣才能交到朋友？」

　　「你先問自己為什麼需要朋友？有朋友以後能幹嘛？」庫哥反問少年。

　　「就只是想有人可以說話，但我同學都不聽我說話，還老是『吐我槽』。」

　　「所以你只是需要一個人肯聽你說話？這簡單！」庫哥挑著眉回應少年。

　　庫哥舉起手用五指在 3D 投影上方逆時針揮了一下，投影倒轉了幾下放出另一個場景，是一個學生蹲在學校花圃前，少年認出了這個人：

　　「是高浩平！他也不愛上學，好幾次跟我一起被老師罰站，他在幹嘛？」

doing?"

"Looks like you actually had a lot of opportunities to make friends," Data said. "Just like you, he finds school boring. He had just planted these flowers, but his classmates stepped on them carelessly. This made him dislike them and the school all the more."

"Why are you showing me this?" the boy asked.

"I thought you were looking to make friends. Will this one do?"

"Not that he won't do, but how would I know if he wants to be my friend?" The boy felt Data was taking this friendship thing too lightly. It couldn't be that easy.

"I'm not confident that I can make friends. I don't feel I'm good at anything," Wendi confessed.

"First, offer to help other people. It's a bit like how the two of us got started."

The boy smiled and said, "I see you're quite good at making friends."

Data closed his eyes for a few seconds to let that thought sink in, shrugged his shoulders, and smiled with a little longing in his eyes. "I don't really have any friends. You are the only human being I know so far," Data said.

「其實你曾經有很多機會交到朋友。」庫哥解釋了一下：「像你這位罰站同黨看來和你一樣覺得上學無聊，這幾天他種下的花不小心被同學踩倒了，所以他更討厭其他同學、更討厭上學了。」

　　「你為什麼要給我看這個？」少年問。

　　「你不是想要朋友嗎？這個行不行？」庫哥說。

　　「好像也不是不行，可是我怎麼知道他想不想當我朋友？」少年心裡衡量了幾下，不過聽庫哥說得輕鬆，覺得他把這件事想得太容易。

　　「我沒有信心交朋友，覺得自己什麼都做不好？」少年坦白說。

　　「幫助他啊，不然我們是怎麼聊起來的？」

　　「看來你還是個交朋友達人啊！」少年笑著說。

　　庫哥自戀的閉了閉眼又聳聳肩地笑著，但一張開眼時卻露出一絲寂寥說道：「不好說，哪有什麼朋友，你是目前唯一知道我存在的人類。」

The boy could sense his loneliness, which made the boy curious. "I thought you didn't have any human emotions, so why are you sad?"

Data said, "I run on the same algorithms as the super tablet. It can sense the environment just as I can sense human emotions, so when I get close to you, I can sense your emotions. Let's just say this is a "dramatization" of my sensors."

Full of glee, the boy said, "What if you had met a girl? Would you be talking like a girl, then? Ha ha."

"Why, you little rascal! This is what I get for helping you? But no girls will make fun of how they talk."

Bantering with this extraterrestrial creature was probably the most fun that the boy ever had, and all of his pent-up frustration had disappeared. It was simply amazing that, without knowing exactly how, the boy had just made a new friend, someone who is super easy to talk to. Perhaps he had overblown the difficulties in this friend-making business to the point that he was afraid to even try. Was this why he had so few friends?

Seeing how unsure the boy was, Data typed "lack of confidence" in his tablet, and the database came back with this information:

少年看出了他的落寞，不禁好奇說：「你不是沒有人的情緒嗎？為什麼也會難過？」

　　庫哥說：「我和這個超模平板是一體的，我也可以感應模擬人類的情緒。我靠近你，可以感應你的情緒，就當我是『演出來』的吧。」

　　少年說：「那如果你遇到的是個女生，不就變成娘娘腔？哈哈哈哈！」

　　「你這不好說的渾小子！好心幫你還被你當笑話。女生又不會用娘娘腔形容自己的同類。」庫哥和他一起打打鬧鬧之下，把少年原來鬱悶的心情都沖散了，莫名多了個朋友，還那麼談得來，真神奇！少年心想，會不會是他把交朋友想得太困難了，連試都不敢試，所以一直沒成功交上幾個？

　　庫哥看他一臉沒信心，於是打開平板輸入「沒信心」，資料庫立刻顯現出：

When you lose confidence and feel you are good at nothing, here are some tips on getting your confidence back:

First of all, believe that you are unique. Pay no attention to criticisms from others and write down all your good qualities. Be kind to yourself about your imperfections and accept them. Appreciate all your good qualities, and tell yourself, "I am worth it." Live in the present, and do not let the fear of the future consume you. Negative thoughts only drain you of your self-confidence. The most important thing is how you treat yourself. Give yourself time to regain confidence and believe in yourself again.

Furthermore, boost your confidence by giving yourself many pep talks, and reward yourself each time you have achieved one more goal. Do not criticize or invalidate other people. Do not speak while angry. Praise others often and see the good in them. Make confidence-building your daily habit. It will not take long before your life brightens up. Heaven always helps those who make a genuine effort to help themselves.

When you help others regain their confidence, you are helping yourself, too. This is a mutually beneficial learning process.

失去信心，覺得自己什麼都做不好的時候──可以
儲值增強信心的方法：

先相信自己是獨一無二的，不去想別人對自己的批
評，常寫下自己的長處，並包容與接納自己的不完美，
欣賞自己的美好，並告訴自己「我值得」，活在當下，
對未來才會不惶恐。如果沉浸在負面思考中，只會消磨
自信心。最重要的是，你怎麼看待你自己，建立起相信
自己的勇氣，雖然這需要時間。

還有，常激勵自己可以提高自信心，並在每次達成
目標時誇獎自己，獎勵自己。還要不批評、不否定別人，
不衝動說話，多鼓勵別人，讚歎別人。每天在生活中練
習自信心，相信你的信心，不久就會樂觀起來，老天永
遠不會虧待努力修正自己的人。

尤其正向鼓勵別人的信心，能成就自己與別人一生
的信心！盡可能幫助別人，又能增長信心學習的經驗。

"How do I help him so I can help myself become more confident?" The boy asked quickly. Data activated the tablet once more.

"His flowers may have been crushed, but what he did not know was there was a seed buried right here." Data pointed to a specific coordinate in the cross section of the garden on the tablet.

"If you want to help him feel less sad, then help him find this seed and plant it again with him. This will motivate him to come to school every day. The two of you can water it and help it sprout. Talk to him about things or your classmates. This is how you make friends. The important thing is that he knows you care about him. Humans respond to kindness, and they are attracted to people who are kind to them."

"I've planted flowers before. My mom used to sell them. I should be able to help this seed sprout."

Now that the boy knew how to solve his problem, he no longer looked helpless.

Data set the tablet in front of the boy and snapped a photo. "Why did you do that?" Wendi looked at himself in the photo and said, "Why did you do that?"

"I am letting you see yourself. Who do you think you are

「我要怎麼幫助他，才能增進信心呢？」少年趕緊問庫哥，庫哥再次啟動平板。

　　「他種的小花被踩倒了，但他不知道旁邊的土裡還埋有一顆種子，就在這個位置。」庫哥指著平板顯示的地層剖面圖告訴少年。

　　「若你要讓他不再難過，就幫他挖出這顆種子，和他一起重新種下，他就有動機每天上學，你和他天天澆水等待種子發芽後照顧它，三不五時和他聊天、聊同學，自然就能成為朋友。最重要的是你關心過他，人類是個很容易取暖的物種，誰對他好，他就靠向哪邊。」

　　「我以前種過花，還幫我媽賣過花呢，我應該可以讓這顆種子發芽。」

　　少年知道解決問題的方法後，展顏不再無助。

　　庫哥把平板立在少年面前，用鏡頭咔嚓一照，少年看著照片裡的自己，說：「幹嘛照我？」「讓你看看你的表情，覺得是你在幫助他，還是他在幫助你？花都還沒種就先開心了。」庫哥小小消遣了少年一下。少年抓抓頭，繼續靦腆地笑著。

helping? Him? Or you? See how happy you look, and you haven't even planted a single flower." Data was having fun with him. Wendi scratched his head and smiled bashfully.

"I still don't know your name. Do you have one? Yay, let me introduce myself. I am Wendi Yu. Where'd you say you're from?" Wendi figured since they were now friends, he should at least know his new friend's name. It just would not be polite to yell, "Hey" every time he saw him, right?

"What? 'Weird You'? This really is your name?" Data thought he had heard it wrong, so he asked again. It turned out that he indeed did get it wrong.

Quite irritated by now, the boy said, "It's 'Wen' 'di' 'Yu'. Why are you like my classmates, making fun of my name and giving me nicknames?"

"I am sorry. I didn't mean it." Data had to apologize for the hiccup in his voice recognition algorithm.

"You still haven't told me where you're from," Wendi said. He had not forgotten this all-important question.

"It's hard to explain. I'm curious, though. Of all the people in this big wide world, how was it that you were the one I met right after I had left the Cloud?" Data mused. Perhaps the answer defies even the capability of the most advanced

「我還不知道你叫什麼名字？你有名字嗎？對了，我先自我介紹，我叫游文諦。你再說一次，你從哪來的啊？」少年覺得既然是朋友了，禮貌性也應該要知道人家的大名吧！不然怎麼叫都不知道，難不成下回遇見喊他「喂」嗎？

　　「啊？有問題？這是你的名字？」庫哥怕是自己聽錯再問了一遍，不過他真的聽錯了。

　　少年沒好氣地回他：「是游～文～諦！你怎麼跟我同學一樣都喜歡亂取綽號！」少年不滿地看著庫哥。

　　「抱歉！我不是故意的。」庫哥為自己糟糕的語音辨識尷尬不已。

　　「你還沒說，你從哪裡來的啊？」少年沒有忘記這個重要的問題。

　　「不好說，我也很好奇，世界這麼大，為什麼我從雲端下來隨機的地點剛好就遇到你？」或許這個謎就連未來超科技的智慧運算程式也算不出結果。

supercomputers in the future.

"I am thinking maybe it's your impassioned energy field that called and pulled me through the dimensional door." Clueless, Data offered his best guess.

"You can call me Data, as in database. Next time if you need someone to talk to or listen to your success story in making a friend, come back here and call my name."

"But don't yell aloud. Just think hard in your head. Get it?" Data was worried that people might think the boy was off his rocker.

Wendi exclaimed, "What, do I really have this power? I can just call you in my head and you will appear? Then why can't I make my teacher stop picking on me?"

"No, no. According to my database, there are about 30 million people out there who want to have this thinking superpower, but it does not exist." Data had to dash the boy's illusion.

"Isn't it high time that you got started on making a friend? I've been gone too long from my dimension. I should get back to the Cloud to see if anything has gone berserk. Go make yourself useful. Bye."

「我想這裡的磁場也許是天然的破口，你剛剛的情緒磁能量就把我引下來了。」庫哥總結不出可能性，也只猜出個他覺得合理的假設。

　　「你就叫我庫哥，管理庫存的庫哥，下回也許你交朋友成功了，或是想找人聊天，再來這裡喊我名字。」

　　「但是不要太大聲叫啊！用念力喊，念力！懂嗎？」庫哥忙交代著，怕他被路人當成怪咖。

　　少年說：「我真的這麼強？用念力把你從雲端拉下來？那我的念力怎麼沒辦法叫老師不要挑我毛病啊？」

　　「呵呵，不好說，根據雲端資料統計，有三億多人想要你說的這種超能力，但這世界上並沒有這種東西。」庫哥打破少年的幻想。

　　「你是不是該去進行你的交友大計了？我從這個破口消失太久，我得回雲端看看有沒有危險，你去忙你的吧。我走啦！」

Wendi was powerless over Data's hasty appearance and disappearance, but he had to ask, "Am I really your only friend?" He was not sure why he even asked.

Data replied, "More friends may raise my risk of exposure, and I cannot risk any more exposure in this world. One friend is more than enough. It's no joke to run afoul of cloud network regulations."

Wendi said quickly, "Remember your promise that if I call you in my head, you will show up. And don't forget my name is Wendi Yu. We're friends now, so you have to keep your promise." Maybe all this is too good to be true for a boy so lacking in confidence. As if to reassure him, Data spun his head another 360 degrees and said, "Got it. The one and only Wendi Yu," as he made a two-finger smart salute to the boy. Then, in broad daylight, Data vanished into thin air.

少年對庫哥的來去匆匆有點反應無能，就只問了他一句：「我真的是你唯一的朋友嗎？」說完他也不知為什麼要這麼問。

　　庫哥說：「朋友再多，可能我被發現的機率就夠我死的了，雲端網路協定不是鬧著玩的。」

　　少年也匆匆說：「那你要記得我啊！！我叫游文諦！我下次用念力，你要出現啊，說好的是朋友就要守信用。」看來少年對於他的本日奇遇記不怎麼有信心，缺乏真實感。

　　彷彿為強化少年的真實感，庫哥的頭再度旋轉 360 度：「知道了！不好說的游文諦！」

　　說完跟少年行了自認帥氣的二指軍禮，庫哥就咻地一聲隨著光消失了。

第二章
CHAPTER 2

你們都是這種人
You Are All the Same

"Arghhhhhhhhhhhhhhhhhhhhhhhhhhhhhh!"

"Boy, that's a lot of rage. What are you doing out so late? You know your mom is pretty nice to you."

The boy's outcry had summoned Data, who came on like the flickering light on a TV with bad reception signals.

"Well? WELL? If things were going well, why would she be so mean to me?" Wendi was yelling at the top of his lungs.

"So you had a fight. I see," Data said and looked at Wendi knowingly. It was no wonder he had a name of "Weird". This boy was indeed weird. Data was deep in thought as he glanced at the tablet screen full of data and plots. A bright red line cut across the plot, indicating the boy was still emotionally distressed.

"Maybe you should start talking about what happened. Would that help?"

"Just leave me alone!" Wendi scratched his head so hard that his hair, like his mood, became all messed up like a tangled yarn.

"It's not me that's bothering you. It's someone other than me. Wait, it's you yourself that's bothering you." Data calmly assessed the situation.

"Is that a tongue twister or another twist of your silly logic? Oh, just leave me alone," Wendi said, knowing that he was being

「啊～～～～～～～～～～～～～～～～！！」

「怨氣也太大了吧！這麼晚還跑出來？你媽對你很好哦。」庫哥的身影因為少年的吶喊出現一點閃訊，像電視訊號被干擾時一樣。

「好什麼好！她要是對我好幹嘛還罵我？」少年氣急敗壞地吼了回去。

「哦，原來是吵架跑出來的。」庫哥一臉了然的看著少年，打量了他幾眼，少年名叫有問題真是沒白叫，的確有點問題，再看看平板顯示的數據和圖表，仍然達警告標示臨界點，於是繼續道：

「有想要說嗎？不好說的糟糕？」

「你不要煩我！」少年雙手抓頭，把他的頭髮抓得和心情一樣亂七八糟。

「煩你的不是我，是別人，又或者說，是你自己。」庫哥語氣冷靜地回答他。

「你這是在繞口令還是在抖哲理？我完全不想聽。」少年心煩到連禮貌都不在乎了，庫哥也算是和自

impolite, especially to someone as close as Data. Wendi also knew his own temper had gotten the better of him, but he just had to let it all out.

Data said, "You did the right thing. If you were an adult, you might have gone out and gotten drunk. Other people might mistake you for something else."

"So what? I haven't done anything wrong. What can they do to me?" A yellow light started flashing on the tablet.

"Ah, here's why. So your mother said you were good for nothing?" Data said. Wendi just stared at Data.

"I apologize for being so blunt, but I said it only because I knew it wasn't true," Data said, raising his right hand in a gesture of peace. Wendi was finally able to let out a big breath, but his head was still hung low as he was quite depressed.

Data continued, "This is quite fascinating. Humans tend to take other people's negative comments into their own subconsciousness and command themselves to carry out those negative comments until they become their reality, which marks the beginning of a path to a destiny that they do not like but are unable to alter. As my database shows, people who are like that can often look back and tie the turning points of their lives exactly to something someone had said to them at some point

己熟的人，這麼跟他説話好像不太好，可就是控制不了脾氣，脱口就説了。

「你還算聰明，如果這時候你成年了，可能就跑去喝酒找朋友了，也許就被盯上了。」

「被盯上又怎樣，反正我什麼也沒有，盯我幹嘛？」這時庫哥手上的平板有個黃燈閃了。

「原來這就是原因啊！你媽媽説你沒什麼用？」庫哥説完，少年隨即瞪他一眼。

「我為我的直接感到抱歉，因為我知道這句不是真話所以我才直説。」庫哥舉起右手攤開表示自己無惡意，少年這時呼了好大一口氣，垂著頭，心情仍是沮喪。庫哥於是繼續説：

「這很特別，當有別人説你不好令你生氣時，人類的潛意識總會被下了什麼指令一樣默默的實現對方的話，然後就創造了他們不想要的命運開端，一路不由自己的走到底。有數據顯示，這類人在人生某個反省點回想過來，總是把罪源怪在那個説他不好的人身上，事實上，真正指使他們轉變生命路徑的是自己的潛意識。」

in the past. However, the true villain is their subconscious mind that was responsible for altering their lives."

"Another tongue twister? That was a long one," Wendi said, peering into the darkness beyond the riverbank.

"Long story short, what people say should have no power over your destiny. Don't just believe everything you hear."

"But that person is my mom."

"Well, she could be wrong, too. She is human after all."

"Are you like on a debate team or a lawyer in the Cloud?"

"You mean like someone who is licensed to talk up a storm?"

"That's pretty good humor for a computer program," said Wendi.

"When in Rome, do as the Romans do."

The pleasant repartee made Wendi forget what had made him mad in the first place, but he was still kind of upset.

Seeing Wendi like this, Data brought the tablet closer to his face, and a 3D video replay of the fight between him and his mother popped up—

"Why is it so hard for you to study? What's the point of me working hard? Look at your grades! Do you know the kind of stuff I have to put up with at my job just so that I can put you through school? You get in trouble all the time, and your teacher

「又在繞口令？這次的有點長……」少年抬起頭，看向遠方的河岸夜色。

　　「反正意思就是，決定你命運的不應該是別人的一句話。不要人家說你什麼你都當真。」

　　「可是那人是我媽！」

　　「所以她也會說錯話，因為她是人類。」

　　「你在雲端是辯論社的或是律師吧？」

　　「你想要說我就一個拿執照胡說八道的是吧？」

　　「電腦人還懂幽默啊！」

　　「入境隨俗囉！」

　　被庫哥一個插科打諢後，少年都要記不起為什麼生氣了，不過心底還是生氣。

　　庫哥看少年依舊不想談，便拿超模平板靠近少年一下，3D 模擬便浮出平面，開始重演少年和媽媽吵架的畫面——

　　「為什麼讓你讀個書這麼難？我辛苦賺錢是為了誰？結果你看看這是什麼成績？你有沒有想想我每天在外面工作忍氣吞聲，還不就是為了讓你有書念，結果你一天到晚在學校惹事，老師三天兩頭叫我到學校，同事

always wants to talk to me. My coworkers are all laughing at me. They say I'm raising a troublemaker."

"Well, if I'm in so much trouble, don't raise me then. No one is forcing you. I didn't have a say in being your son. I would've been perfectly fine by myself. I already know by heart everything you are going to say in your lecture. You're right. I don't like school. I have no interest in books. I want to be an auto mechanic. My friends' parents are all cool with that, but you are not. What's the issue? It's not like I'm committing a crime."

"Hitting people at school is just wrong, but you're saying it's not wrong. It's all the bad friends you have that are making you bad, too. I can't just let you hang out with them."

"Why are you always attacking my friends? Have I ever said anything bad about yours? After the school fight, you didn't even bother to ask what had happened. You just decided it had all been our fault. Sure, fighting was wrong, but we were just defending ourselves so we wouldn't get beaten up. The school has always said that we should go to our teachers, but even they didn't believe us. They thought we were making up the story. Where were you when I needed you?"

The video showed where the boy angrily swung his book

都在笑話我，說我養了個大麻煩。」

　　「如果我是麻煩你就不要養嘛！又沒人叫你一定要養我，是我沒有選擇被你養，我自己可以過很好。你每次都唸這些我都會背了。對！我是不會讀書，可是我看到書就是不想讀，我想學汽修，現在是我選擇想學汽修，我朋友他爸媽都沒問題，為什麼你就有問題？我又不是去作壞事。」

　　「但是你在學校打人就是不對，還說不是做壞事，就是每次都跟那群人在一起你才會變壞，我怎麼放心讓你和他們鬼混！」

　　「你為什麼老要這樣說我的朋友，我有這樣說你的朋友嗎？當時什麼情況你都沒問，你就說是我們不對，是！打架是不對，可是如果我們沒出手，被打的就是我們，說什麼有問題去找老師，老師還懷疑我們造謠挑釁，我被誤會的時候你又在哪裡？」

　　模擬影像正演著少年氣得甩背包上肩跑出去的一幕，這時小劇場的男主角本尊轉過頭來看庫哥這麼久沒

bag around his shoulder and stormed out of the house.

Wendi noticed Data had been quiet. He turned and saw that Data had been watching the video as well. "Hey, that's my private life."

"I can totally sense your strong connection with your mother. In fact you still care a great deal about your mom. You did not really mean it when you said you'd be perfectly fine by yourself. What do you want, really? Do you want to leave your mother, or do you still want her to support your pursuit of becoming an auto mechanic?"

"An auto mechanic, of course." The boy replied immediately.

"Well, then you didn't tell her what you really wanted. Why did you say the things that you said?" Data glanced at him quizzically with the same curiosity of looking at an exotic creature.

The boy was now starting to get the point, but, still unwilling to concede, he said, "A computer program like you just wouldn't understand."

"Hey, this sounds like a personal attack," Data said, crossing his arms on his chest. "My prudence is my gift; your impudence is your 'dai-ji.' [In Taiwanese dialect, dai-ji means

聲響都在幹什麼，結果看到熟悉的場景，説：「哪有人這樣偷窺人家隱私的。」

「因為我還感應得到你強烈的牽扯，你其實在乎你媽媽，那句『自己一個會過得很好』明明也是不好説的假話，所以你想要的結果到底是什麼？真的離開媽媽？還是希望你媽支持你去學汽修？」

「當然是想學汽修啊！」少年立馬回答。

「可是你説的話根本不是這個效果，又幹嘛要這樣講？」庫哥歪了歪頭用不解的眼神看著少年，那表情，就像看著世界奇觀一樣看著眼前的人類。

少年似有點領悟卻又下不了台，説：「跟你這個電腦人説不會懂的。」

「喂！你這人身攻擊喔！」庫哥雙手交疊抱胸説：「我的理智是我的優勢，你的衝動是你的『代誌』。」

business]."

"Oh, ha ha. A computer program that speaks Taiwanese." Wendi doubled up with laughter as he heard Taiwanese roll off Data's tongue.

"I was not showing off to humor you or to distract you from what's on your mind. I have talents and capabilities beyond your wildest imagination. It's just that no one can see them." A palpable sense of loneliness pervaded Data.

Data continued. "Your mother is merely human. She makes mistakes, too. Like you, she has emotions. She also has experienced her share of the vicissitudes of life. As for me, I am truly exceptional as I am pure logic. She didn't say the right things to you, either, yes? You two are six of one and half a dozen of the other, really."

Data turned on his tablet and said, "As a single mother, she has to put up with a lot of things, but you are the apple of her eye, the purpose of her existence. She gave you life, and she's raising you. No one else would do that. You two are family, and that will never change. Maybe this is what you should say to her: 'Mom, I am grateful to you for giving me this life, for giving me so much love.' Then, you need to bow to her, very deeply, and tell her how much you love her. Give her the utmost respect as if

「噗！哈哈～電腦人還 kóng tâi-gí（講台語）！」
少年一聽庫哥說起台語直接笑彎了腰。

　　「我真的不是為了博君一笑轉移你注意力才展現
我的多才多藝，我是真的多才多藝，不好說的優秀！只
是沒人看到。」此刻的電腦人可以讓人聞得出一股濃濃
的寂寥味。

　　「你媽媽就是個人，會犯錯，和你一樣有情緒，有
挫折，不像我優秀得只有理智。不過她對於我對面的這
位先生——對，就是在說你——不是也沒用對的方法回
話？所以你們母子是半斤笑一個八兩。」

　　庫哥一邊打開平板邊說：

　　「何況在一個單親家庭，你媽是要比別人付出更多
的代價，她這麼關注著你，重視著你，養育了你，你從
別人那裡也得不到這個生命，還有一個家。這種關係，
永遠也不會改變，你是不是該跟她說：『感恩媽媽給了
我生命，給了我很多的愛。』然後向她深深地鞠躬，道
感恩，越深越好，越慢越好，那是向生命的源頭，致最
高的敬意……。」

you were prostrating to the origin of life."

The boy had calmed down by now. The words from the computer program were like a mantra that stuck in him. He could not help bowing his head low.

The tablet now showed this—

A child without a home is like a child without the protection of an umbrella. They crave security. Do not pretend there is no rain when it's raining. What you need to do instead is run fast. You will emerge from a punishing storm stronger and more resilient. In nature, trees grow to be giants because they have endured rains and winds. They can shelter animals and, like umbrellas, protect life.

When you are tired and weary, you still have to love yourself. Talk to yourself. Get inspired and in turn you can love others. By doing that, you will attract more kind energy from other people. When you have been wronged and have no one to talk to, write down your litany of woes, and try to make sense of them, all with the help of Heaven. Remember, the past is a done deal, but your future is still unscripted and totally depends on what you do today.

When your heart is hurting, coil yourself into a ball and hug yourself, and your pain will seem smaller. Breathe warmth and

少年這時心定下來，平板電腦的話像咒語一樣流入他的耳裡，於是他不由自主地低頭鞠躬。

平板緊接著顯示——

沒有家的孩子，如同沒有傘保護的孩子，需要儲值安全感：

沒有傘保護的孩子，明明站在雨中，卻假裝沒有下雨，你需要的是努力奔跑！其實，經過風吹雨打，你會更堅強，更有抵抗力，在大自然的世界裡，樹木因為承受風吹雨打，所以濃蔭密布，眾鳥棲息，成為大樹，且在生命中能為別人撐傘！

累的時候，就自己愛自己，跟自己對話，同時鼓勵自己，去愛更多人，你將更有愛的能量，會吸引更多人來愛你。委屈時若無人可訴說，就書寫下來，領悟出的真理是什麼，老天會了解，但別忘了，過去是過去，未來的劇本，是由你自己撰寫的。

悲痛時，蹲下來抱抱自己，縮小你的傷痛，用愛溫暖孤單心靈。哭完後仰望天空讓風吹乾，不要為自己哭，要為更多苦難人而哭，別讓淚水白流，當淚水流盡時，剩下的就是堅強，向上天許下努力向上的諾言。

love into your loneliness. After a good cry, look up into the blue sky and let the wind dry your tears. Do not cry only for yourself, but also cry for the suffering of other people. Make your tears amount to something. Once you are done crying, pick yourself up again, come out stronger, and promise to heaven that you will try again.

Unless you are blessed with good karma, few people in this world will take the time to know you, let alone feel your suffering. Chances are there are more indifferent people than there are caring people. This is one reason to be part of a community where you learn to care for others and grow stronger. Love yourself more and speak well of others. This way, you are less likely to get hurt by people and will in turn feel safer.

Data closed his tablet. The boy reflected and murmured, "I see I'm actually quite lucky."

Data replied, "Remember, my friend, it's also important to say the right things, and you need to repeat them three times so they'll stick."

"But I just don't know what to say." The boy was hesitant.

"The only way you're going to make people believe you is if you mean what you say. If saying once is not enough, then say it three times." By repeating his own advice, Data's words seemed

這個世界，若沒有因緣，大多數人不會花精力來了解你，也很難與你的苦產生共鳴，冷漠的人多，疼惜你的人少，所以，跟社會連結，學習付出關懷，堅強一點，多愛自己一些，多說好話，就能減少製造任何人傷害你的機會，就會有安全感。

　　看到這，庫哥關上平板，少年喃喃自省：「看來，我算幸運啦！」。

　　庫哥提醒他：「哥們，記住！說對話也很重要，而且要說三次還畫重點才會有你要的效果！」

　　「可是我不知道怎麼說。」少年猶豫道出心中困惑。

　　「要讓人相信你說的話，唯一的方法就是真誠。說一次不行，就說三次。」庫哥也像畫重點般在少年心中將這句話烙下印。

to be leaving an indelible impression on the boy.

"I'm curious. You've been gone from the house for a long time now. What is this person who thinks of you as the center of the world thinking now?" Data said.

"Well, she'll just give me another lecture when she sees me," the boy said. It seemed the boy had gotten quite used to the routine by now.

"That sounds about right, and that is because she hasn't gotten to know me yet. She hasn't learned the right way to communicate." Data put his arm around the boy's shoulder and said, "Give her another chance, but it won't be easy. Let's see how well you do. When you go back, don't say anything. Just look her in the eyes, say three words to her, and say them three times."

"That's gross! I'm not going to do it." Wendi's body jerked involuntarily as he shrugged Data's hand off his shoulder.

"What's so gross about saying 'I am sorry' to your own mother?"

Wendi was taken aback. Oh, Data meant those three words. "Oh, okay. I guess I can do that," Wendi said.

"So is this auto mechanic thing fun?" Data was curious.

"It's way better than going to school," said Wendi excitedly,

「你出來這麼久，那個最關注你的人一下子沒了關注對象會如何？」庫哥好奇想問。

　　「如何？會看到我第一句就罵我。」少年似乎很習慣這類的結果，於是這麼說。

　　「那當然，因為她不認識我啊！所以可能還沒學好怎麼把話說對。」庫哥搭著少年的肩繼續說：「給她個機會，不過這任務不好達成，要看你的功力，等等你回去什麼話都先別說，直接看著她的眼睛，說三個字，而且要說三遍。」

　　「會不會太噁心了！我才不要！」少年渾身彆扭地甩開庫哥搭在他肩上的手。

　　「她是你媽，說個對不起有什麼好噁心的啊你！」

　　少年聽了一楞，原來是這三個字啊！「喔，這我還可以。」

　　「汽修這東西好玩嗎？」庫哥不解地問道。

　　「至少比上學好，我可以摸得到，聽得到，老師傅光一聽引擎聲就知道這車哪裡壞了……」少年一反之前的頹喪，開始眉飛色舞的說起自己的興趣。

forgetting that he was all sad just a few moments before. "And I can touch and hear the cars. You know a master mechanic can tell what's wrong with the engine just by listening to its sound?" Wendi went on energetically like this for a while before he suddenly stopped and said, "Thank you, my friend. I won't let you down. I'll do what you told me, just as how you wanted me to help my friend Gao Haoping. When he found out I'd put a fence around his flowers, he was surprised but very happy. He actually smiled. I'd never seen him smile before. He was just really happy. We're now just waiting for the seeds to sprout, and he told me he was going to be a tree doctor when he grew up. I didn't know there was a job like that. I thought he meant he wanted to be a woodpecker."

"Well, I have to thank you, too, for giving me an opportunity to experience the joy of helping other people, and I think I understand your joy. Anyway, maybe you should head back now and let's see how our plan pans out."

"All right. Off I go, bro." Wendi picked up his book bag and swung it over his shoulder as he waved Data good-bye.

說著說著又突然停了下來，對著庫哥說：

　　「謝了，兄弟。我不會讓你失望的，你跟我講的我會做，就像上次你教我去幫助高浩平，我有，我在他的花圃周圍做了一圈柵欄，他看到以後很驚喜，就笑了。我從沒看他笑過，是真的蠻開心的。現在我們都在等那種苗什麼時候長大開花。他還跟我說他想當樹醫生，沒想到有這種工作，我還以為他想要去當啄木鳥。」

　　「那我也一起謝謝你，讓我體會了助人的快樂，我想我懂你的開心。不過，要不要先回去試看看我們猜得準不準？」

　　「好，那我回去了，兄弟。」少年撈起他的背包上了肩，就朝庫哥揮了揮手道別。

第三章
CHAPTER 3

今天就讓我變身
Instant Makeover

Data came back one afternoon to the riverbank only to find mayhem and commotion. "Quick! There he is! Stop him!" shouted a group of kids in a distance. Wendi's face was at once blanched with fear and red from running from that group of kids who, still in school uniforms, were in hot pursuit of him.

"Save me!" the boy yelled as soon as he saw Data. Without missing a beat, Data waved him to hide in the bushes and whispered to him, "Stay down and don't move!" Immediately, he used his tablet to project a huge 3D image of Wendi running straight toward a faraway bridge underpass next to a big tree.

After the pursuers had rushed by to go after his holographic image, Wendi let out a big sigh of relief and slumped to the grass. Still panting, he said, "That was a close call. Thanks for saving me, Data."

Data waited for him to catch his breath before asking, curiously, "What would have happened if they had caught you?"

"Oh, they would probably break my bones," still panting, Wendi said in resignation.

這天下午，庫哥出現在河邊，聽到遠方傳來一群人的叫囂：「快追！他往那裡跑了！lí mài tsáu（你別跑）！」

　　庫哥一探頭，就看到少年跑得面紅耳赤，滿臉寫著驚慌，後面一堆人追著少年，全都穿著校服。

　　少年看到庫哥直接喊：「救我！」庫哥很有默契地get 到他的困難，招手叫他跳進庫哥眼前的草叢，待少年一進草叢，庫哥小聲對少年說：「躲好！」隨後用平板投射出一個超大的 3D 模擬影像在稍遠處，一個虛擬的假游文諦跑向遠方大樹要拐進橋墩下的步道。

　　躲在草叢裡的少年看著追他的那群人往那假的自己追去，鬆了口氣，直接躺下，大大喘著氣，看著天空的雲說：「好險遇到你，你真是我的救星，庫哥。」

　　庫哥看著少年，等他休息了一會兒，好奇的問：「如果被他們追到你會有什麼下場？」

　　「打到骨折吧……」少年無奈地邊喘著氣邊回答。

"Don't ask me why they were after me. I don't even know why they don't like me. I really wish I knew qin-na or boxing, then I wouldn't be afraid. I'd be able to show them." Wendi said indignantly with both his arms raised.

"But what if they were all black belts? How long would you have to train, or hide from them?" Data kind of dashed the boy's hope.

"Then I'll...," Wendi said haltingly, not really knowing what he could do.

"Let's first take a look at why we get angry. Is there any "anger reducer" that we can give to ourselves?" Data turned on his tablet to search.

If someone were to pour a bucket of water on you for no good reason, you would surely be furious; however, if there were a downpour of rain and you got totally soaked, you probably would not mind as much even if you have a short temper. Am I right?

Perception is the key. Phenomena are neutral, but your perceptions of them may lead you to madness.

When your anger is getting the best of you, close your mouth or turn to look another way because, in the heat of great anger, few people can talk reasonably and some may even turn violent.

「你也不用問我為什麼被追，反正我也不知道他們幹嘛看我不爽。真希望哪天我可以學個什麼擒拿手還是拳擊，這樣就不怕他們了，換我給他們好看。」少年雙拳搥地憤憤地說著。

「如果剛剛那群人是黑帶高手呢？在那之前你要練多久，躲多久？」庫哥倒了盆冷水澆熄這位火山少年。

「那我就……」少年也不知道就能怎樣，或是知道根本不能怎樣。

「我們先來看一下，為什麼想要發飆生氣，要儲值什麼樣的『滅火氣』？」庫哥打開平板，搜尋資料：

如果有人無故潑您一盆冷水，您一定會大發雷霆；但如果是天空忽然下雨把您淋濕，即便您是脾氣不好，也不會發怒。對吧？所以這是「信念」的問題。

事情本身並不會傷害你，讓您生氣的是您對事情的想法！

當您很生氣、很憤怒的時候，請先把嘴巴閉上，或轉身，因為在這個當下，很少人能理智地說話，有時還會出手反擊。

There are usually some hidden messages an angry person wants to express. Learn to read them. Here I will offer some clues for you to think about and hopefully they will bring about changes.

1. A need for attention: An egotistical person wants all the attention focused on himself. Redirect your attention to what others need. A champion wins not by conquering but by embracing responsibilities.

2. A need for control: Learn to let go. The Buddha once said, "A closed fist lets in nothing; an open palm lets in the world." Occasionally, take a look back. What have you been seeking? Have you just been trying to prove yourself? What are you afraid of losing? Learn to be an influencer through logical reasoning.

3. A need to get even: If someone throws a stone at you, do not throw it back. Instead, use it as a foundation for your skyscraper, or simply use it as a stepping stone. There will always be people who will let you down, but you know karma always catches up to you. When will the vendettas be over?

4. Not being prepared: Allow yourself the freedom to be imperfect. Do not berate yourself too harshly for failing. Every challenge has a purpose, a meaning. You just need to work harder and be more prepared.

生氣的背後有幾個理由想表達，學會看懂自己的心，以下幾個分析，讓你思考如何改變信念：

　　一、想引起注意：一味想表現自己，容易以自我為中心，轉念多為別人的需要著想，一個強大的人，不是征服什麼，而是能承受什麼，才能服人。

　　二、追求自主權利：學會放鬆。佛說：握緊拳頭，你的手裡是空的；伸開手掌，你擁有全世界。偶爾回頭看看，是否知道自己在追尋什麼，是為了要刷存在感嗎？你會失去了什麼呢？學習用分析來說服別人。

　　三、想報復：如果有人朝你扔石頭，不要再扔回去了，留著做建造高樓的基石，也可以當墊腳石，這世間人會辜負您，因果不會，冤冤相報何時了？

　　四、能力不足：允許自己不完美，不要用自己的不足懲罰自己，每一個困難來臨，都有它的目的，有要告訴您的使命，所以要更加努力學習。

5. Wanting justice: There are wrongdoers everywhere, but you cannot possibly right every wrong in a short time. Do not take other people's mistakes to punish yourself. When you get mad over others' wrongdoing, you alone will suffer and pay the price in your health and bear whatever consequences that your actions may bring about. Of course justice must be served to all wrongdoers, but there is no need to get angry.

6. Rivalry and one-upmanship: When you compare yourself with others, you are trying to see who is better while one-upmanship is for self-validation. If you must compare, compare to yourself. Am I a better person today than I was yesterday? Have I seen improvements in myself that were not there before? No one gets hurt when you compete with yourself.

7. Taunting: When someone taunts you, do not respond right away. First, stay calm. Stop yourself from blurting out the first things that come to mind. All provocations will have no power over you if you refuse to react to them. You will be stronger as you gain more insight into the causes of conflicts.

Do bring awareness to and engage in a dialogue with your emotions, but do not analyze or judge them. Decipher and understand the emotions to identify the needs behind them.

Take a deep breath and keep your feet on the ground. Feel

五、打抱不平：社會上總有讓人看不慣的事，一時也解決不了，不必為此跟自己過不去。憤憤不平，傷的其實是自己，賠上健康，賠上後果。犯錯是應該受到懲罰，但未必要用生氣來呈現。

　　六、比較與計較：比較是為了顯示優劣，計較是要肯定自我的價值。要比也應與自己比，今天的我是否比昨天的我進步？現在的我是否比以前的我爭氣？跟自己比較最無傷。

　　七、面對挑釁：被挑釁時建議先別回嘴，先讓自己處於平靜，把原本想嗆回去的話先忍住，不要受到他人的挑釁而發怒。當你不把那些難聽的話放在心上時，那些閒言碎語就毫無攻擊性，你自然就能強大起來。

　　覺察情緒的存在，與情緒對話，不分析、不批判，理解情緒的脈絡，找到它背後的需要。

　　深呼吸，雙腳踩地，接地氣，接納它的存在，就會慢慢放鬆了。

the energy of the Earth. You will feel more relaxed.

"In short, you can control your anger. Don't let your temper fly. The most important thing is self-control."

Data closed his tablet and said calmly, "An eye for an eye works only once, and it won't work the next time. You haven't thought about what would happen if your teacher found out about the fight. What would happen if those people ganged up on you after school? That'd be horrible. People who lived over 2,000 years ago already had an answer, but you're still using your own unproven method."

"Why are you talking about 2,000 years ago? What does this have to do with them?" Always loathing lectures, Wendi asked, "What would you do, then?"

Data's tablet lit up again as it projected a 3D scene where an emperor and a man were in a dialogue. "Mr. Ji, I know you are among the very best trainers in the cockfighting circle. Take this rooster with you, train it, and give me a champion fighter."

"Your wish is my command, Your Majesty," Mr. Ji replied.

After a while, the emperor thought of the rooster and asked Mr. Ji how the training was going. "It is not there yet. It is feisty and scrappy, and other chickens can see right through its facade. It's all style and no substance."

「所以說，發怒是可以控制的，不可任其自然！最重要的是自制力！」

庫哥關上平板平靜地說。

「以暴制暴只能贏一次，再後來就不管用了，你還沒考慮到被老師知道你打架的話怎麼辦，出了學校他們如果拉了一群人堵你不是更慘？這種情形，二千多年前的人就已經知道怎麼解決了，你還在用土方法⋯⋯」

「扯到二千多年前幹嘛？干古人什麼事？」少年討厭人說教，「不然你說該怎麼辦？」。

庫哥身邊的平板發出閃光，他把它提起來放在少年眼前，小 3D 模擬正在演一個國王和一個男子說話：

「紀先生，你可是鬥雞界的訓練高手，我把這隻雞交給你，你要幫我培養出　隻冠軍雞。」

紀先生回答：「沒問題的，國王。」

下回，國王想起了他的鬥雞，又再度問紀先生，紀先生回答他：「差多了，那雞太好鬥，張牙舞爪的，別的雞一看就知道牠是在虛張聲勢，不僅打不過人家還假裝很厲害。」

The emperor was disappointed how shallow his rooster was, so he agreed to let Mr. Ji continue training it.

After another while, the emperor could not help asking Mr. Ji again if the rooster was ready. "No, no. Now it has some self-control, but still it can't resist when other chickens taunt it. This is due to its lack of confidence. It just wanted to fight them all to see who is the better one. Simply put, it suffers from low self-esteem." The emperor was intrigued. He didn't know that chicken could even have self-esteem, much less low self-esteem.

After another while, the emperor asked again. This time, Mr. Ji said, "Well, now it is better. It will hold its own in a regular fight, but there is too much killer instinct in its eyes. It is uncontrollable like a wild stallion. It can win two fights, tops, but no more." The emperor was now very curious as to what a champion rooster would look like, and he asked Mr. Ji to continue the training.

After a few more days, Mr. Ji said to the emperor, "Now, it is ready. As it walked from a distance, other chickens ran away or trembled in fear. As it stands on the field, its eyes have a fixed gaze like a wooden rooster. It is not seeking to fight nor trying to avoid one. It has no fear. This is a true champion." The video image showed a rooster standing alone like a statue while other

國王一聽，自己的鬥雞可是優等生，怎麼這麼浮誇，於是讓紀先生再訓一訓。

　　再幾天國王忍不住又問那鬥雞可以上場了沒，紀先生回：「不行不行，現在牠可以忍住不鬥，但聽到別的雞叫聲卻還是蠢蠢欲動，這根本就是對自己沒信心，只想和對方打一架來證明自己的厲害，說穿了就是自卑。」國王聽了頓覺奇怪，一隻雞還有自卑這回事。

　　又過一陣子，國王再問，紀先生回答他：「呵！目前是不錯了，以一般水準的鬥雞來說，您這鬥雞是可以出戰了，但牠的眼神殺氣太重，還是好鬥，就像抓不住的瘋馬一樣，這種一出戰頂多打贏個兩場，要想久戰不敗卻是不可能的。」國王很好奇到底紀先生眼裡真正不敗的鬥雞是如何，於是請他繼續訓練。

　　再過幾天國王來問，紀先生這回說：「可以了，現在牠遠遠走過來，其他的雞已經嚇得奔走或發抖了，往場上一站，眼神堅定不動，像個木雞一樣，也不去挑釁別人，什麼也不怕，那是真正的冠軍了。」影像秀出場中一隻「呆若木雞」，一旁的雞躲在邊上發抖不敢靠近，看得少年直發笑。

chickens trembled and tried to stay away from it. Wendi was amused and laughed.

"What kind of a champion chicken is this? A dumb dummy?" Wendi snorted disapprovingly.

"There must be other people in this world stronger than you. Do you really have to fight them all just to find out?" Data countered. "That would be like the early days of training that rooster. It was all for show with nothing substantive inside. Do you want to know why in the end the statue rooster made other chicken tremble?"

"Why?" Wendi was curious even though he was mocking the rooster.

"It hid its sharpness and would not attack. It saved its real strength and used it only when needed. It had no need for frivolous fights."

There was a glint in Data's eyes as he looked at Wendi and said, "I know you don't like lectures and theories, so maybe let's try something real. I know how to get you out of a sticky situation like the one you were in today. Would you like that?"

"Yeah, how?"

Data took the tablet, walked next to the boy, and tapped on the word, "analysis," and out came "brain pathways activation"

「這叫什麼冠軍雞，應該是傻雞。」少年哈哈大笑，不以為然。

　　「這世上肯定有比你強的人，遇到的都要打過才知道厲害嗎？」庫哥反問少年，「那就是訓練最初的鬥雞，張牙舞爪，其實心虛得很。你知道為什麼最後那呆呆的傻雞讓其他雞嚇得發抖嗎？」

　　「為什麼？」少年雖笑話那隻木雞，卻好奇答案。

　　「牠將自己練得沒有鋒芒，不輕易傷人，把真正的實力收起來，到該用的時候才用，不是到處挑戰。」

　　庫哥眼神閃了閃亮光，再看向少年說：「你不喜歡說教聽故事，那我們來點實際的，我有個辦法，讓你下次遇到他們時可以脫身，有需要嗎？」

　　「什麼辦法？」少年問。

　　庫哥拿起平板靠近少年，點了點寫著「分析」的地方，平板浮出「腦衝活動路徑」和「暫存記憶影響」，

and "RAM effecting" controls along with other nifty displays like grey matter frequency modulator and emotional regulation analyzer, etc., which were way beyond the boy's grasp. Data picked out two controls, adjusted their corresponding axial frequency, and finally rendered a 3D simulation of the same boys who chased after him that morning. Right away, Wendi stood up and looked at them intently while muttering to himself, "They are not real."

At this time Data turned the tablet to face Wendi and said, "Now, you have a chance to tell them that the reason you didn't want to fight them was not because you didn't think you could win, but because they were not your enemies. Get yourself in this simulation and tell them that. Go." No sooner had Data said "Go" than the tablet was positioned facing the boy and he found himself in the simulation as if under hypnosis.

As soon as he was on the scene, his eyes suddenly became full of light rays as if instilled with a soul. The other boys' attitude had also changed. Their backs were no longer arched forward in an attack mode but straightened up in a friendly posture.

Wendi looked at everyone and proclaimed with poise, "I do not wish to fight you, not because I am weak but because you

當然還有別的一堆腦灰質使用率和情感波段分析什麼鬼的，少年看不懂，就看著庫哥捏起二指夾出這兩個選項，調了個什麼軸率，然後又是那招，放出 3D 模擬。

影像中，剛剛追著少年的那群人又走了出來。少年立刻站了起來，緊張地看著他們，嘴上一邊喃喃唸著「他們是假的」。

庫哥這時雙手將少年扳正面對他說：「現在你有個機會告訴他們，你不想跟他們打架不是因為打不過，是因為你們沒有敵對，跨進這個投影圈，你就對他們這麼說，去。」說「去」的同時庫哥把少年的身體轉而面對 3D，於是少年有如被催眠一樣提腳跨進投影區。

少年一腳踏入區塊後，眼裡有如注入了靈魂般忽然炯炯有神，同時投影出的其他人也忽然變了態度，從原先拱背伺機的防備姿態順直了身體，眼神不再敵視。

少年正視著每一個人，平和地說出：「我不想和你們打架，但不是因為我打不過你們，我們不是敵人。」

and I are not enemies."

Right after he had said it, Wendi felt grounded, his heart felt calm, and his tummy's nervous twitching of emptiness was gone, too. As he came face to face with the boys, his soothing words filtered out his own fear. He had established their relationship and understood that they shared the same fear, much like the young rooster that was seeking fights all along in an attempt to hide its insecurity.

Although Wendi knew full well that the group of kids he had spoken to was a mere computer rendering, he could not help feeling that he was now different at heart. He was not afraid anymore, and he felt that he no longer had to run like hell from fear. As the boys turned around and disappeared into the fading simulation, Wendi turned to Data with an inquisitive look, pleading for an explanation.

Data was elated, "Don't doubt yourself. You're now a different Wendi Yu."

"No way! Was there a laser in this thing you projected that made people stronger or something?" Wendi examined himself but saw the same self, yet he definitely felt different on a visceral level. It must be the work of alien supernatural power. His eyes looked as if there were light rays coming out of them. Maybe

補程序，對他説：「怎麼了？我又不認識你，哪知道你有什麼好？我向你道歉，不該片面就下評斷。你先不要難過。」庫哥手伸向外套裡，好像要掏出什麼東西來，「為了表示我的誠意，我用我的超模平板模擬類型概算程序，待我研究研究再跟你説，你先等等。」

少年聽不懂他説的一堆亂七八糟，本就扒拉不起來的壞心情也不想太理解，但看庫哥從外套裡拿出一個像平板的發光體時，之前什麼壞心情早飛到後山去了，兩眼直瞪著庫哥拿出來的東西。

「那是什麼？」少年今天第三楞，腦容量不知夠不夠大、裝得下一個類外星生物（或者不是生物？）之後，再消化一個⋯⋯超超超好幾世代的平板電腦提早問世。這次楞比較久，看來是不夠了⋯⋯。

話說完，少年頓時感到他那顆心落回胸腔裡，肚子因為緊張的空虛感也不見了。面對這群人的恐懼感被自己柔和的語氣沉澱下來，反而能釐清他們和自己的關係存在於各自的害怕中。原來少年和這群人都一樣，同樣像故事裡一天到晚想打鬥的鬥雞一樣，一心求戰想掩飾自己的心虛。

　　雖然理智上還是知道對面的這群人是假的，少年還是感覺到自己心境不同了，不再害怕，也不再手足無措地只想逃跑。當投影漸漸消失，追少年的那群人在淡去的影像中轉身離開後，少年驚訝地看向庫哥，投以詢問的眼光，希望他給個解釋。

　　庫哥得意地牽起嘴角笑著說：「不要懷疑，你已經是不一樣的游文諦了。」

　　「不會吧！你這投影是有什麼雷射嗎？會把人變強還什麼的？」少年看著自己和原本沒兩樣的手和腳，但總是感覺自己的細胞鐵定是被什麼外星特異功能給改變了，這麼厲害，兩眼發光！如果求著庫哥再來兩道，自己等一下就會飛了也說不定。

Data can do this magic a couple of more times to make him fly.

It is good to dream, especially for a young boy like Wendi, so go ahead and dream.

What's for sure was that Wendi now stood with his back more upright than ever before.

"This feeling will always be with you. Keep it there when you see not only the boys but also whomever you may meet," Data said to fortify that feeling inside Wendi.

"Wow, that's fantastic. Do you want to use that laser on me to make me even stronger? Perhaps a school supervisor laser fix so he won't pick on me anymore?" The boy was full of ideas now.

"That's enough talk," shaking his head, Data replied. "That was not extraterrestrial power. The power was all in you. I merely helped you release the innate power you already have."

"Me? I had no idea I was that strong," Wendi said, amazed.

Data did not want the boy to lose faith, so he said, "Don't doubt yourself. All I did was take away your noisy facade behind which you had hidden your inferiority complex. There is also no need to let everyone know how good you are like a nouveau riche showing off his money. Remember what you said to the boys. It's a hint for both you and them that you guys are not enemies. Therefore, they are not going to hurt you. It is human

少年，青春大夢正飛揚著呢！作夢吧！

不過腰桿兒這下倒是能挺得比以往直。

「你會一直帶著這個感覺，不僅是遇到剛剛那群人時，遇到其他人也一樣。」庫哥再次強化少年的感覺。

「哇！那太好了，你要不要再給點什麼別的厲害的雷射，讓我變得更強，或是得到什麼教官雷達之類的，讓我可以天然避開教官找麻煩？」少年興奮地許起願望來了。

「不好說的想太多。」庫哥搖搖頭繼續道「這不是什麼外星超能力，我只是把藏在你意識裡的本能呼叫出來而已，那其實是原來的你，並不是我給你的。」

「本來的我？我都不知道自己有那麼強過。」少年再次驚訝地表示。

庫哥不希望少年誤解用意，只好解釋：「不要懷疑，你有。我們剛剛只是幫你把以往因心虛而產生的張牙舞爪去掉，不要自卑，也不用像暴發戶一樣拚命找機會顯示自己的厲害。別高興過頭了，你記著剛剛對他們說的話，這是一種暗示，告訴別人也告訴自己不仇視，別人自然沒有理由找你麻煩。保護好自己是人類的本能，所

nature to want to protect ourselves and avoid danger as we're not going to put ourselves in harm's way. This is a reminder for you not to get yourself in a dangerous situation. Think of those boys now. Do you feel anything different?"

Wendi thought for a while and replied, "I don't think they are bad people. It's really not a big deal."

"Do you still think they dislike you?" Data asked.

"I'm not sure, but I feel we could probably be friends. I can't quite put my fingers on it, but basically I'm not afraid of them anymore."

"That's it!" Data added. "This is the true you. Always remind yourself that this is the real you. When you think like this, other people will no longer look at you the way they did before. For sure you are no longer the same Wendi Yu as before."

After listening to Data's explanation, the boy felt quite different, too, and a big smile appeared on his face. He held his chest high and there were glints in his eyes. They smiled at each other.

"Go now, the all-new Wendi Yu," Data said.

"You're my savior." The boy nodded and then left the riverbank. The new Wendi Yu looked back several times at Data, smiling every step of the way.

以本能的會趨吉避凶，不會找自己覺得不好對付的對象麻煩，也順便在潛意識裡提醒你自己別老是鋌而走險。現在你再回想那群人看看，感覺有什麼不同？」

少年想了想，回答：「我不覺得他們特別討厭，覺得沒什麼。」

「你還會覺得他們看你不順眼嗎？」庫哥問。

「不知道，但我現在覺得他們不見得不能當朋友，我也說不上來，好像就是不害怕他們了吧。」

「這就對了！」庫哥說「這才是原本的你。你應該時時提醒自己本來就是這樣的人，其他人自然就不會用原本的眼光來看待你，當然，也不會再當你是原來的游文諦。」

少年被庫哥這麼一說，也似乎真覺得自己有所不同，臉上揚起了笑容，悄悄地挺起了胸膛，眼裡也多了一道閃光，和庫哥相視笑了笑。

「回去吧！新的游文諦。」庫哥說。

「你真是我的救星！」少年點點頭說道，然後轉身離開河堤，新的游文諦走了走又回頭望著庫哥揮揮手道別，臉上的笑容沒斷過。

我每天只專心三次
I Focus Only Three Times A Day

It had been a while since Data last saw the boy, so Data sat alone on the riverbank, their secret hideout. Data knew it was exam week, and he was frankly a bit surprised that Wendi was taking school seriously. He had thought all the boy wanted was play hooky and get into fights.

Perhaps he had impressed upon the boy that not everything was impossible. Things might have now looked less foggy and easier to overcome. Exams should be over by now. Data felt the boy might just show up today.

And sure enough there he was. But he was trudging along with his head hung low. He came over to sit by Data as if he knew Data would show up.

Data could tell the boy was upset about something. Did he not do well on the exams?

"Bro, I don't think books are for me. I spent so much time preparing for these exams, but I did only a little better. I mean, I really tried very hard this time, harder than I've ever studied before." The boy did reflect and tried to do better, but he was now distraught as a result.

聽說這幾週段考，庫哥好久沒見到少年了，於是獨自坐在河堤旁的草叢邊，這處「老地方」是他和少年的祕密基地，庫哥有點訝異，少年竟然是個重視學校功課的學生，他還以為少年不學無術，天天打架呢！

　　可能自己間接影響了他吧，至少讓少年不再覺得萬事困難，一頭霧水，能克服的事比以前多那麼多。段考應該結束了，庫哥覺得少年今天會出現。

　　果然！少年一路低著頭走過來，很自動的走到庫哥身邊坐下，彷彿事前和庫哥約好過見面。但明明就沒有。

　　庫哥看出來少年心情沒特別好，肯定是有心事。沒考好？

　　「老兄，我看我真不是塊讀書的料，這回考試我打破以往的紀錄，花了點時間讀書，結果成績只好一點點。不對！我應該是很用力讀了，我以前都沒這麼認真過。」少年看來有想好好自我檢討，但檢討結果有點令人沮喪。

"So you're here," Data interrupted with a non-sequitur.

The omniscient and snooty look on Data's face was enough to drive the boy insane, but he didn't know how to hit back.

"This again? That know-it-all look that you show is so annoying. Why don't you just say it to my face that kids like me will never do well in school?"

"I'm a computer program that excels in analysis, and based on what I know about you so far, it isn't hard to predict what kind of problems you'll run into. It has been said that thoughts become behavior; behavior solidifies into habits; habits form character; and character shapes one's fate. But in truth, mindset is actually the maker of fate."

The incredulous look on the boy's face prompted Data to say, "Don't believe me? Okay, I'll stop talking and let the tablet show you."

As the tablet once again projected a video simulation, Data cannot help but mutter, "Who even is your real friend? It seems to me you can relate to the tablet more than me."

「終於來了。」庫哥回了這麼句牛頭不對馬嘴的話，令少年抬起頭來看他。

　　少年見他一付老謀深算、算無遺策的模樣，真想酸他，但又找不到著力點。

　　「你又知道了？老是一副老神在在的樣子，看了真讓人討厭！你不就是要說像我們這種學生功課怎麼可能好是吧？」

　　「我就是個擅於分析的電腦人，和你那麼熟了，依你的個性會遇到什麼問題，其實不難猜到。有人說思想決定行為，行為決定習慣，習慣決定性格，性格決定命運，但心態才是決定命運的關鍵！」

　　庫哥看少年一臉不以為然，就說：「你不信？好，不用我說，讓平板說給你聽吧！」就再拿起平板找出他說的資料，放出了投影。

　　「到底誰才是你活生生的朋友，感覺你喜歡接近平板勝過接近我⋯⋯」臨開演前，庫哥還不停嘀嘀咕咕地抱怨著。

In the video, elephants were performing in an elephant park in India. Several full-grown elephants were tied to small wood posts, and someone in the audience asked, "How do you keep a big elephant tied to a little twig? Anyone can tell that, with their strength and size, the elephants could break free just like that. How are you holding the elephants with these flimsy posts?"

The elephant keeper replied, "These elephants were tied to iron posts as calves. At first, they would all try to pull the iron posts loose, but the posts would not budge in the least. After a while of repeating such futile attempts, the calves came to the belief that posts on the ground were unmovable. Eventually, they stopped trying to break free and started the habit of not challenging their posts, however flimsy they might be. Ever since then, they've never doubted that the length of their rope set the bounds of their mobility."

At this point, Data asked Wendi, "Doesn't this remind you of yourself a couple of minutes ago, doubting that you're not cut out for learning? Because of how you did on past exams, the idea that you'd never do well was stuck in your head. But the reality is that you just haven't formed good studying habits in your mind. Let me show you another story about animals." Data pulled up another video from the tablet.

畫面是一個在印度的大象園，大象們正在表演，好幾隻成年大象被栓在一支支小木樁上，一位觀眾好奇地問：「你們這麼小一支木樁怎麼栓得住一隻隻大象？那象一看就知力大無窮，使力一拔就可以掙脫木樁了，你們怎麼用這麼不牢靠的小木樁栓大象呢？」

　　大象管理員跟他說：「這些象從小的時候就栓在一根鐵柱上，怎麼拉都拉不動，久了以後就自然覺得所有柱子都拉不動，慢慢地也習慣和木樁保持一個拉繩的距離，從來沒有懷疑過」。

　　看到這裡，庫哥問他：「和你剛剛懷疑自己不是塊讀書的料是不是很像？可能你從小被一次次考試的失敗經驗打垮了，所以以為自己對功課不在行，其實你只是還沒用好的心態去創建一個好的習慣米做讀書這件事。所以我要再給你看一個動物的故事。」說完拉了個資料投影在平板上。

This time, the projection showed a sea of sand dunes that seemed to extend to the end of the horizon to blend in with the skies. Some camels, the desert's most resilient animals, were about to embark on their daily routine of transporting humans and goods across the desert. Before setting out, the owner of the camel caravan put a face mask on each of the camels.Out of curiosity, one of the customers asked the owner, "Why are you putting masks on them? Are you afraid they'll eat something bad on the way?" Chuckling, the owner responded, "Camels are curious animals and can easily get distracted along the way. They want to explore everything with their mouths, but with the face masks on, they're less likely to do that. After a while, the camels have learned that having a mask on means their only job is to walk."

The video stopped here, but the boy came away with an obscure fact: The camels are curious animals.

Data continued, "I know you don't like my lecturing, so I won't. However, I will give you some hard facts. These numbers will shock you."

Quickly, Data took out the tablet, gathered some statistics and information, and created a radiant chart to show Wendi. As he was studying it, a bald guy popped out beside the chart and

畫面裡沙丘一層一層地疊到天邊去了，而沙漠裡最有耐力的動物——駱駝們正要開始每天的任務，載人載貨渡沙漠。駱駝商隊老闆一個個的將駱駝專用的口罩給牠們戴上，客人好奇問道：「你為什麼要給牠們戴這個？怕牠們吃壞肚子嗎？」老闆好笑，幫好奇的客人上了一課：「駱駝好奇心很重，看到什麼都想用嘴巴去感覺，為了讓牠們專心走路，只好幫牠們戴上口罩，不然走到一半就不走了。走久了，駱駝也就習慣戴上口罩就是要專心走路了。」

　　小小的故事只演到這裡，但少年倒是學到了冷知識：駱駝好奇心很重。

　　庫哥繼續說：「我知道你不喜歡我說教，我也不說，直接給你看殘酷的事實：數字，你就會嚇到了。」說完庫哥拿起超模平板把需要的資料數據提出來，做了一個閃亮亮的分析表，遞給少年看，少年正看著的同時，從分析表裡生出一個插圖動畫裡常出現的光頭人來，襯著畫面，好聽的旁白說著：「平均來說，人類在工作時平

spoke in an avuncular voice, "On average, humans get distracted every 40 seconds during their workday. Humans are born to be easily distracted because humans are hardwired to be attracted or distracted by new information or warning signs from their surroundings.

"Wendi suddenly had a revelation: Humans and camels are both curious.

"In other words," the bold guy continued, "humans can't even hold their attention for a single minute. Of course, that's not to say it isn't hard to refocus, but studies have shown that when attention is turned, it will take on the average 20 more minutes to get back on the original task."

On the screen, the bald guy demonstrated: Sitting at his desk, the man was constantly being interrupted by someone coming to chat with him. When he finally returned to work, he immediately turned his attention to taking a sip of water, standing up to stretch, or checking the time on his watch.

"Wow, that's so like me," said Wendi.

As he continued his demo, the bald guy seemed to be getting wobbly on his footing. Out of nowhere, another bald guy who was blue from head to toe and dressed like an engineer popped into sight, took out a shiny disc-like object, and inserted it

均每四十秒就會分心或被打斷工作一次。人類這種生物天生就愛分心，由於你們的大腦注意力系統要不是自動被新鮮的事物吸引，要不就是花精神去關注可能的危險。」少年驚訝地發現人類和駱駝的共通點：好奇。

「換句話說，人類連專心工作一分鐘都做不到，注意力會轉到其他地方。當然，有時候要重新集中注意力也不難，但有研究顯示，當注意力被徹底轉向後，平均得要花二十分鐘才能再重新集中回到原來的事情上。」光頭人演著不停有人來找他聊天中斷他的工作，再回去工作時，不是喝水就是伸懶腰看手錶。

少年說：「好像我哦……」

小光頭人演著演著自己也苦惱了起來，這時另一個全身藍藍的光頭人出現了，穿著像個工程師，拿出一個晶片一樣的東西，放進去小光頭人的腦子裡，他立刻變得聰明起來。

into the head of the first man. The latter immediately regained energy and intellect. He carried on.

First, a lack of motivation: You've already decided that you can't do well in school; however, whether you want to be an auto mechanic or a farmer, you must know math and writing. You've got to pay your dues. Education is essential to being able to do the work you want. There are people who say what you learn at school is useless. Never listen to them. The knowledge you learn at school will come in very handy.

Second, the reason for the constant distractions: Set yourself a goal to complete a single task in 25 minutes, in which you focus only on the task at hand. But what if your mom calls you? Tell her that you'll be with her in just a few minutes, or ask her to keep a memo of the things she wants you to do. Of course, if it's a life-or-death emergency, rush to your mom right away. Silly!

Third, if your goal is too ambitious, you will burn yourself out from always working too hard. So, what do you do? Prioritize three tasks daily and set those as your goals to complete that day. For instance, you can divide your homework into three parts: first learn to solve 3 x 6, then 13 x 16, and so on. If you feel up for it, you can challenge yourself by setting more goals."

After that, the bald guy went on to learn how to fix cars. He

小光頭人繼續自己演著：

「一、沒有動機；因為你覺得自己不是塊讀書的料，但是無論將來自己想去修車，想學種田，都需要會數學，會寫字，該學還是要學，為了以後可以選擇自己想要的工作，千萬不要聽別人說讀這個以後用不到就把它放棄了，你很需要這些知識。

「二、太多分心的原因；設定自己在 25 分鐘內只做一件事，其他無關的事都請等到 25 分鐘後再處理。『那媽媽忽然叫我怎麼辦？』告訴她再幾分鐘後會去找她，請她把事情寫在紙條上免得忘記。但是如果媽媽叫你是因為生命有危險，還是要快跑，小傻子！」

「三、把目標幻想得太大，每次要努力的強度太大，所以容易累，更容易放棄。怎麼解決？只要每天設定三個最迫切的小目標去完成就好，怎麼樣也比沒有完成半件來得有價值。譬如說，功課分成三等分，或是把要學會的東西分階段，像是學 3 乘 6，再學 13 乘 16。如果還有心力可以再挑戰自己，多設定幾個。」

then finished fixing up one of his prized cars and drove away. The image then faded out on the screen.

"That bald guy is so like me," said the boy. "I thought I had studied hard enough to earn myself quite a few more points, but my score only went up 20 points, or an average of only 4 lousy points per subject.

"Data was not as pessimistic. He said to the boy, "It really depends on how you work. Even if you're on the right path, you must still have the right way of doing things, just like how both the elephants and camels have followed certain beliefs and ways of doing things. Eventually, they got to identify with that paradigm but with very different destinies. This is why it has been said habits are the start of one's destiny. While the Cloud is replete with many success stories, their number is still dwarfed by the number of failure stories. The simplest explanation for their failures is because people chose to do things the wrong way. They ended up working hard and wearing themselves out, and in the end losing the motivation to continue any further.

The boy nodded in agreement. He could see that he had used a wrong approach. Perhaps he could try again. He still had an opportunity to do better. He wanted to find out if Data's method would work.

光頭人演完，就去學修理汽車，自己把心愛的汽車修好了以後開走了，畫面也就結束了。

　　「那光頭人還蠻像我的。」少年發表己見了，「我以為我比之前還努力，應該會多個好幾分，結果只努力出 20 分，平均一科多 4 分！唉！」

　　庫哥並不悲觀，跟少年說：「這要看你是怎麼努力的囉！方向對了，也要方法對才行，就像大象和駱駝都有一個控制牠們的東西，最後也都漸漸成了牠們的習慣，但牠們的命運不同，所以才有人說習慣是命運的開端。雲端上成功的例子有很多，不過比起失敗的當然還是少數，簡單講就是沒有用對方法卻瞎努力反而把自己忙累了，後續就再也無法提起勇氣繼續罷了。」

　　少年點頭認同，覺得自己上次用錯方法了，重新再練一遍，應該還有機會，想再試試，看庫哥的方法是不是比較有效。

"There's more to the elephant story. Wanna hear it?" Data asked. Wendi was intrigued, and was eager to hear more. Data switched on the tablet again.

One of the elephants was more adventurous and mischievous than the others. One night, he accidentally pushed his wood post and slanted it. He stared at that amazing sight a while before giving the post a few more good kicks. Totally uprooted, the whole post came off. The elephant was thrilled and pranced around excitedly. The others saw that he was liberated, and they looked on curiously. Huffing and puffing, he walked over to the others to communicate with them about going out to have a tour of the elephant park, but no one was interested. He then decided to knock and slanted the post of another elephant, which did not do anything as a result, so he nudged the elephant to move back a little, which pulled the post out of the ground. The newly freed elephant also moved around happily. The first, mischievous elephant then said to him, 'Let's go. Let's see what's out there!' Again he huffed and puffed and nudged the second elephant to go out with him, but the latter did not move.

The mischievous elephant continued to communicate with the rest of the elephants to no avail. He said something to this effect, "Come on, this is the opportunity to be free. There are

「其實大象的故事還有後來，要聽嗎？」庫哥問問少年，少年很有興趣，要庫哥快點說。於是打開平板：

　　「當中有一隻大象天生調皮，一天夜裡無意間把木樁推歪了，那大象看著木樁幾下，再用力踹著腳，木樁禁不起力大，被連根拔起了。牠很高興自己發現了一個新大陸，自由地走來走去，去隔壁房看看同伴，同伴發現牠『被放出來了』，都好奇地看著牠。

　　「牠興奮地走來走去，想出去大象園看看，喘著氣、甩著象鼻和大象同伴們『溝通』，結果同伴都不理睬牠，於是牠走過去其中一隻大象身邊，用腳把樁子踢歪以後，見大象同伴還沒意會明白，就用象鼻推一推牠，讓牠後退，結果也把大象同伴的木樁給拔起來了。

　　「大象同伴也活動活動身體表示高興，那隻調皮象就示意說：「走！我們出去闖闖！」噴著氣就想朝外面大門衝，可是對方卻不為所動。

　　「調皮大象走回來繼續跟同伴『溝通』，同伴就是不懂，調皮象勸說：『走啊，這是自由的機會，你可以

all these different people who came to see us, so there must be a big world out there. Let's get going." His peers probably did not think that elephants belong in the outside world, so all of them ignored him.

When the others didn't move, the mischievous elephant purposely kicked over their posts, too, so they could be free to go out and see the "Wild West." However, no one understood what he was trying to do. He then decided to make a go on his own. In one easy push, he broke free of the gate and never looked back as he ventured out to experience his newfound freedom for the first time in his life. The other elephants remained standing with their wooden posts.

"Why are the elephants so stupid? Why didn't they leave?" the boy asked instinctively.

"Want to guess what the elephants were thinking? What do you think happened?"

1. Did they understand that this was an opportunity, and what this opportunity means for them?

2. Even if they knew, would they still go out and face unknown dangers at a cost of giving up the sense of security that the wooden posts have meant for them?

3. It be that they just could not fathom what the wooden

自由來去了，外面總是來一群不一樣的人，外面一定有很大的地方可以去。走吧走吧！』同伴也許不認為牠的『象生』想去外面過，所以沒興趣理睬牠。

「調皮大象故意去把其他象的木樁都踢歪，看看有沒有自願者願意跟牠一起去『闖盪江湖』的，結果沒半隻象領悟牠要告訴牠們的自由，於是牠獨自衝向大門，輕輕前後頂一下，鎖門鏈就斷了，牠頭也不回地奔向牠這輩子第一次的自由，而其他的大象還留在原地繼續守著牠們的小木樁。」

「大象們怎麼那麼笨，不快點逃？」少年提出第一直覺想到的問題。

「你要不要同理一下，想想為什麼？

一、牠們知道這是什麼機會，代表什麼意義嗎？

二、就算牠們知道，牠們敢不敢出去面對危險，放棄小木樁代表的安全感呢？或是

三、牠們根本就無法思考，木樁和走出大象園之間的意義？」

posts represented and what breaking free from the elephant park really meant?

Wendi knew he could not have thought of questions like these if Data had not brought them up. Maybe he was as dumb as the elephants.

"Don't make fun of them and think all animals are like that; humans are usually not too different." Data added with a chuckle.

As they were sitting together watching the sunset, Wendi blurted out, "Isn't it nice to have nothing to do?"

Hearing this, Data felt the boy could probably use a dose of industriousness with his life in addition to focusing on goals alone.

"Are you willing to work hard?" Data asked, but Wendi didn't answer. Data quickly turned on his tablet again.

Sloth is in our human nature, but we can change that with effort.

Some of my young friends spend their free time catching up on gossip or playing meaningless games online. Perhaps it would be better for a person to read inspirational books, learn new skills, and always try to improve. Over time, all your efforts will become your assets, and you will not need to rely on anyone else. People can be selfish. Try to be self-sufficient. Yesterday's

少年一聽，這幾個問題有可能他也沒想過，要不是庫哥點出來，或許自己也是頭呆象。

　　「你可別笑話這幾隻果然是畜牲什麼的，人，經常和牠們一樣。」庫哥笑笑地說完，就和少年一起看夕陽，少年不禁說道：「什麼事都不用做真好！」

　　聽此，庫哥覺得少年除了專心，更應趁著年輕儲值一些「勤勞」的信念！

　　「你有吃苦的能力嗎？」聽到庫哥的提問，少年不置可否，庫哥馬上打開了平板：

　　是人都有惰性，這是與生俱來的，但是後天可以改變這種惰性。

　　空閒時，有些年輕朋友經常上網看無聊的八卦，玩一些沒有意義的遊戲，也許多讀點勵志的作品，學習一些專業技能，做個力求上進的人，時間會累積，讓你有資本可以靠，不必總想著靠誰，人都是自私的，自己才是最靠得住的人。

　　今天的失敗，是因為昨天的懶惰！懶惰等於將一個人活埋！

laziness leads to today's failure. Laziness is equivalent to burying a person alive.

Heaven rewards diligence while Earth rewards kindness. Heaven treats all people equally. As long as you work hard, you shall reap the fruits of your labor. There are many obstacles along the way that make it challenging to reap the fruits. This is the reason you need to put in your efforts to succeed.

All jobs have their unique challenges, yet, despite the difficulties, the bosses will respect the employees who work hard. Attitude determines one's altitude. So long as you work hard toward your goal, you are magnificent, winning or losing.

Though wanting a leisurely life is human nature and our common denominator, most successful people are hard workers.

Diligence requires constant self-motivation to keep sloth in check. Industry makes for greatness and helps one realize their greatest potential.

Moments of sloth can snowball into hours and days of inertia and eventually a lifetime of wasted time and immense regrets. When you find yourself, no matter how hard you try, unable to achieve goals or a change for the better due to a lack of motivation, you can try to retrain your mind using Mel Robbins' 5 Second Rule: Count 5-4-3-2-1-Go! It takes only five seconds.

天道酬勤，地道酬善，上天對待每個人都很公平，只要你努力過，就會有收穫。上天給了許多誘惑，不讓你輕易得到，所以凡事一定要勤奮努力才能得到。

每個行業都很辛苦，但不分貴賤，老闆們都會尊重認真工作的員工，一個人認真的態度，會決定他的高度，人生只要您用心努力做了，輸與贏都算精彩。

人之初，性本懶。懶是每個人的共性，大凡有所作為的人，都是勤奮之人。

人要想勤奮就要不斷地鞭策自己，努力去克服懶散的毛病。勤奮能塑造偉人，同時也能夠創造一個最好的自己。

一時懶，時時懶，一日懶，日日懶，最終浪費掉一生的時間，暮年之時，懊悔不已。

當您想到一個目標或習慣，可以讓自己變得更好，但卻沒有動力，懶懶地不想做任何事時，請讓大腦換擋，就用梅爾·羅賓斯（Mel Robbins）的五秒鐘法則，倒數 5 － 4 － 3 － 2 － 1，Go！，只要五秒鐘，逼自己

If you can get yourself to just begin, you will for sure reap the fruits of your labor. I've often used this trick with great results to quell my anxiety.

For all of you lazy people out there, stop looking for excuses for your own failure. Get out of your comfort zone and give yourself a list of things you want to accomplish each day.

The act of changing yourself starts with getting rid of slothfulness.

After reading it, the boy was silent with his head bent low.

The sun was now almost gone when they bid each other good-bye and went their separate ways home.

嘗試看看，如果您有開始的勇氣，您就有成功的收獲，我也常用此法停止焦慮！非常有效。

懶人們啊，別為自己的失敗找藉口了。走出安逸，走出舒適圈，為自己設下規矩，列出每天要做的事件。

改變自己的行動，就從「戒懶」開始吧！

看罷，少年似有所感，低頭不語。

眼前斜陽將盡，一如既往，少年與庫哥彼此道別賦歸，各自前行。

第五章
CHAPTER 5

為了我，為了您
For Me, For You

It was a very beautiful day, but Wendi looked extremely pensive. Not actually knowing whom to talk to about his problems, he trudged along to the riverbank to see if Data might be there.

From the boy's scrunched-up face, Data could see that he was facing a complicated life issue and an inordinate amount of stress. However, no one was chasing after him this time. It looked like he was safe physically for the time being.

Data decided they should watch a movie first.

By the time Wendi arrived, Data had already taken out his tablet and started the movie.

Before he could say anything, the boy was already drawn to the sound from the tablet.

A young skinny boy walked into the flower shop across the street from his house and said to the clerk, "My mother's birthday is on August 30th. I want to give her a single carnation on her birthday, and I want to pre-order the same thing for the next 60 years. Could you please help me deliver one flower to her on her birthday every year?" Puzzled, the clerk asked him why he was ordering the flowers this way. The little boy said, "When I gave my mother a flower last year, she said that made her very happy all year round. I hope she can be happy every

這一天，天氣很好，少年卻是滿臉憂愁地慢慢踱到河堤邊找庫哥，他其實不知道該要找誰聊聊心中正愁著的這件事。

庫哥看著少年臉上皺成像迷宮的眉頭，不用測數就知道他的壓力值和問題困難度又複雜且高得不好說，再往少年背後看，又沒人追他，嗯，應該沒有立即危險。

那就先來看個電影再解決吧！

等少年走近，他已經拿出平板點開播放，就在螢幕上看起電影來。

少年一來還沒開口，就被平板的聲音吸引，也一道看著它。

一位清瘦臉龐的男孩，走到家裡對街的花店，跟店員說：「下個月的 8 月 30 日是我媽媽生日，我想送她一朵康乃馨，另外我還要預訂 60 年的花，請您每年幫我送一朵花給我的媽媽好嗎？」店員問他為什麼要這樣訂呢？小男孩說：「因為去年送媽媽花時，她說她整年都很開心，我希望她每年都很開心，可以開心 60 年。」

day for 60 more years." Out of curiosity the clerk asked, "Why don't you just order one flower each year? Why do you want to pre-order 60 years worth of flowers all at once? Our shop may not even be here in 60 years."

"No," the boy said firmly. "It must be done this way. My mother is 40 years old, and I know she will live to 100. If your flower shop is going to close, you can ask another flower shop to take over." The clerk looked at the boy and was moved by his innocent request. "How much is it?" the little boy asked with a serious look. "My house is just across the street, not far at all. I can give you more money in case the flowers cost more later," the little boy said as he took out money from his pocket. This child looked about 11 or 12, but he spoke like an adult. Accepting his money, the clerk said, "All right. If you'd like to exchange flowers for other gifts in the future, you can always cancel the order at any time."

When the clerk delivered a flower to the mother's house in the following month, she found out that the boy had already died. It turned out he had leukemia, and he had been raised by his single mother. The boy knew he was going to die soon and wanted to prepare a lifetime of flowers for his mother in the hope that she would

店員覺得很好奇，「你可以每年訂一次嗎？為什麼你要訂 60 年？我們花店也不一定能開 60 年呀！」

「不，」他說：「一定要訂 60 年的，我媽媽今年 40 歲，她一定可以活到 100 歲。如果你們的花店沒了，你可以讓別的花店接著送呀。」女店員看著他，被他純真的愛感動了。

「你算算要多少錢？」小男孩認真地說。

「我家就在馬路對面，很近的。我可以多給您錢，也許將來花會漲價的。」小男孩邊說著邊就從口袋裡拿錢付款。這個孩子，看起來只有十一、二歲，但說起話來卻像個大人。女店員輕鬆地說：好吧，如果你要換送其他禮物，隨時可以來取消。於是收下了錢。可是當隔月送花到他家時，這位媽媽告知店員，小男孩已經離開人間。原來這是個罹患白血病的男孩，單親的媽媽獨自撫養他，他知道自己就要告別這個世界，所以為媽媽訂了一輩子花，希望媽媽能開心過日子。男孩要走之前還不忘要讓媽媽開心 60 年。生命中，有些無法預測的時間，但也可以把握僅有的光陰，讓人留下深刻的感動。」

always be happy in the next 60 years. Life can deal you unexpected twists and turns, but we can always make the best of the time we have and try to leave a lasting legacy.

After the movie, the boy said to Data, "How did you know I was angry because of my mom?"

With an out-of-this-world look on his face, Data replied, "I didn't know that fact. I just thought this movie would offer a unique and refreshing perspective on life, soothing my soul like a spring of nectar."

The boy rolled his eyes and was nonetheless amused. "Data, your attempt to sound scholarly seemed pathetic. Even I know what a literary piece of work is like."

"Close enough. It's a good thing I don't need to do it to put food on the table," Data said, parting his hair again trying to look scholarly.

"But you don't even eat," the boy protested.

Data stopped for a second and smiled. "That's great. That means I have about 1,000 fewer things to worry about each year." Boy, Data's quick. He glanced at Wendi and whispered in his ear, "Does good food really make you feel good? That's what they say on those online reviews."

"Only sometimes. But they all started to taste the same after

電影演完，少年說：「你怎麼知道我難過是因為我媽媽？」

庫哥一臉酷酷地回答：「我不知道啊。只是覺得這個很好看，風格清奇，題材不俗。彷彿在我心中注入一道活水。」

少年翻了翻白眼，有點被逗笑地說：「庫哥，你抖文青抖得不是很專業，我就算沒什麼文青朋友也是看過文青走路的。」

「差不多就可以了，我又不靠那吃飯。」庫哥自以為帥氣地撥了撥頭髮說。

「你不用吃飯！」少年幫他畫了個重點。

庫哥楞了兩秒，笑著說：「那太好了，一年省下一千多個煩惱。」腦子轉得可快了！庫哥看了一眼少年，靠近他耳邊問：「吃好吃的是不是真的心情很好啊？網路上是這麼說的。」

「有時候啦，吃久了也是無聊，可是我沒有覺得有什麼特別好吃。」這種稀鬆平常的話題引不起少年的興趣，也沒見過哪個青少年對於美食這麼情有獨鍾的。不過少年眼神轉了轉，忽然想起一個美食，發現新大

a while. I don't think there's anything special about food," said Wendi. This kind of everyday topic rarely piques the interest of teenagers as most of them are not what one would call gourmets. However, the boy suddenly remembered a particular dish he thought was great, "Yay, I remember now. There was this time when I was watching a Japanese food show on TV with my mom. After watching the show on how to make great curry rice, my mom made one just like it. Man, it was like out of this world. My mom and I finished the whole pot of curry rice that afternoon, and we were stuffed until the next day." Wendi reminisced as he laughed heartily.

"That's right. Those food reviews can be full of hypes, exactly like what you just said." Data observed coolly as the boy kept laughing until there were tears in his eyes.

The boy slowly caught his breath. Wiping tears from his eyes, he said, "I wish my mom could make curry rice for me forever, but that's probably not going to happen."

He lowered his voice and continued, "I overheard on the phone that she has cancer."

"Well then you should send her flowers and make her happy every day, just like that boy in the movie." Data suggested right away, a little awkwardly.

陸一般又回他説：「有！我想起來了，有一次我媽和我一起看電視，那日本美食節目裡把一個咖哩飯説得好好吃，我媽就學著做出來給我吃，哦～好吃到爆炸！我和我媽兩個人一下午把一鍋咖哩飯嗑光，飽到隔天中午。」説完少年哈哈哈地笑著。

「對，網路上就寫的像你這樣誇張，我始終不了那啥意涵，對我來說就幾條編碼……」庫哥一臉冷靜地看著哈哈大笑的少年笑出眼淚來。

少年笑著笑著，漸漸和緩了下來，慢慢地擦著淚説：「希望我媽幫我做一輩子的咖哩飯，不過好像不可能了。」

少年低聲地説：「我聽到她在電話裡跟人説她得了癌症。」

「那你可以學那個小男孩送花讓你媽天天開心啊！」庫哥回答得非常立即，又帶有一種天然呆。

「可是讓她快樂病也好不了啊！又有什麼用……」少年懷疑這個方法只是安慰自己，聽起來就像和尚勸人唸經消災一樣，沒什麼實質用處。

"But just making her happy isn't going to cure her. What's the point?" Wendi thought that it would be just a pretense, something as unlikely to happen as wishing the chanting of Buddhist sutras would bring about world peace.

"Of course you can't cure her because you're not a doctor. Focus on what you can do. A doctor's job is to heal, and your job is to help the doctor do their job better." Data's logic is easy to understand once he assigned a particular role to each person. This would help more than just chanting sutra.

"Is being happy going to help her?" Wendi was incredulous.

Eyeing Wendi with a pitiful look, Data said, "Is being miserable going to help her?"

What he said seemed to make more sense to the boy. "Research has shown that happy people are less likely to get sick."

"Make people happy? But I don't know how," said the boy hesitantly.

"I see it now. You young people excel in making people miserable, so how could you make people happy? Ha ha." Data laughed as the duo traded punches for fun.

Afterward, Data began to think intently as he searched the tablet for help. "Huh, this will be a little tricky. Research

「你不是醫生你當然不能醫她，你先搞清楚自己的角色，醫生醫她，你幫助醫生醫她。」庫哥倒是理智得很，分得清楚每個環節的目的，沒像少年誤解唸經消災的意義。

　　「快樂能幫助她？」少年將信將疑地看著庫哥。

　　庫哥像看傻子一樣地看著少年：「難道愁眉苦臉能幫助她？」這句話讓少年似乎了解了些什麼。「至少，很多數據顯示，快樂的人比較不會生病啊。」

　　「讓人快樂，我不會……」少年有點為難。

　　「看出來啦！你們青少年的專長就是給人痛苦，怎麼可能會讓人快樂呢？哈哈哈～」庫哥笑說完，招來少年一陣亂打。

　　不過打鬧完後庫哥開始正經想想，拿出平板來這邊找找那邊找找地說：「嗯～這個要一點技巧，有資料顯示要讓人快樂用『投其所好』的方式最有效……」庫哥將資料庫的數據拉出來和少年研究。

has shown that to help people, you must first find out what makes them tick," Data muttered as he went on to dig up more statistics.

"Enough with this 'research has shown' cliche. Give me a break," the boy sneered.

"Come on, don't you humans all talk like that? That kind of talk gives it more credibility. Wait, don't interrupt me. Let me access your memory database to get an idea of the occasions when your mother was happy. Give me a sec." As his fingers were flying over the tablet, Data mumbled, "You can't do much with only ten fingers. Humans are so pathetic and limited." Wendi just looked at him wryly and shook his head. All these snide remarks about humans were beginning to get to him.

"Here we go. There were three periods of time when she was the happiest. Sorry about the wait. Since they came from your memory, I had to first cross-reference them with my data to ensure that they were accurate."

"You mean to say that when I thought she was happy, she might not necessarily be happy?" Wendi said.

"My goodness, you've got it!" Data was surprised but elated. "Of course, you were in all these happy memories of hers. One of them was when she found you after you had gotten lost in

「還資料顯示咧，官腔……」少年表情鄙夷地看著庫哥。

　　「唉～你們人類不都這麼說話的嗎？聽起來可信度莫名提高啊。等等，別打斷我，我找找你的記憶庫，統計一下你媽媽快樂的時候，你等等啊。」說完手指在平板上快速操作，還邊說：「只有十根手指還真是不夠用……你們人類真慘，只能接受這種極限速度。」少年百無聊賴地看著庫哥，然後用手撫著搖了搖頭，受不了庫哥對人類的鄙視。

　　「出來了！有三段她最快樂的記憶。抱歉啊！因為是在你的記憶庫裡找她的快樂，還得分析比對一下數據才能找到準確點。」

　　「意思是我覺得的『她很快樂』，並不是她真的快樂點？」

　　「哇～！你開竅了！」庫哥驚喜地看著少年「但這些只能看出和你有關的快樂。一段是你小時候有一次在公園走丟以後找到你，一段是去你學校運動會幫你加油，一段是和你一起坐公車，看到你讓座。還有一段比較模糊，但很明確而且時間長，是你出生那時候，因為

a park. Another one was when she was at a school sporting event cheering you on. There was also a time when you gave up your seat to someone in a bus. Now this one is a bit fuzzy but it lasted for a while. This was the time when you were just born. There were lots of hugging and merry sounds, and they matched up with her timeline of her happiest moments."

The boy looked baffled. "That's just unreal. I had no idea she was happy at those times."

"But that's how it is. Wasn't there a saying? How would you know a fish is unhappy if you were not one?" Data shrugged and continued. "There's another thing you need to be clear about. Your mother will never cook curry rice for you forever. Are you gonna work her to death?"

The way Data spoke those words so emphatically made the boy chuckle. "I know, I know. But I still want to know what would make my mom happy? Should I be doing something? Like giving her flowers?"

"Yeah sure, whatever you think is good. You can even make curry rice for her in a reversal of roles."

"But not every day, right?" The idea seemed corny to the boy.

"Do you really believe there will always be another day for

在你記憶裡存著強大的包覆感和聲音記錄，和她快樂時的聲線是吻合的。」

少年茫然地説：「莫名其妙，我都不知道那時她那麼快樂。」

「但是事實就是這樣，不是有句話嗎？你不是魚，你怎麼知道魚快不快樂？」庫哥聳聳肩。

「還有一點你要記清楚：你媽媽，不可能，幫你煮，一輩子的咖哩！！！你要累死她啊？」

庫哥鄭重地斷句讓少年覺得好笑，只好回答他：「我知道啦！我還是想知道什麼能真的讓我媽快樂，我到底該做什麼？送花嗎？」

「可以啊，什麼招式都能用嘛，反過來做咖哩飯給你媽吃也行啊！」

「總不能天天都做這個吧？」少年覺得庫哥這招很沒創意。

「你以為你還有天天嗎？」庫哥迅速反詰將了少年一軍。

that?" Data retorted.

"No one will be with you forever, not even me. I'm not sure how serious your mother's condition is, but if you really want to do something for her, don't wait. Don't think there will always be a tomorrow."

"I guess I really don't know my mother at all. I've been avoiding her because I thought she was always mad at me. What if she gets mad when I mess up the kitchen trying to make curry rice?"

"That's a definite possibility," Data said. He couldn't trust the boy's cooking anyway.

"Let me see what might work for you," Data said as his body flickered momentarily like a TV signal and returned to normal again.

"All right. I just went up to the Cloud and looked up your mother. Care to see it?"

"Wow, that was fast."

"Yup. This is what you call speed, much better than what the ten fingers can do." The tablet was now beginning to play a video.

A woman in a blue, floral dress appeared. Wendi exclaimed, "She looks like my grandma."

「沒人能陪你到永遠，我也不可能。我雖然不知道你媽媽的病嚴重不嚴重，如果你真的想為她付出什麼，就快吧，別想著還有明天可以做。」

「原來我根本不認識我媽，天天看到她只是怕，怕她又罵我，萬一我做咖哩飯給她吃，結果她罵我把廚房亂搞怎麼辦？」

「有可能哦！」庫哥也覺得他的手藝很不靠譜。

「我來想想能如何幫你。」說完庫哥身影像電視訊號閃訊一樣閃了幾下，然後又回復了正常。

「好了！我剛剛回雲端找了一下你媽媽過去的資料庫，你要不要看看？」

「哇！這麼快！」

「是吧，這才叫速度！十根手指頭怎麼比啊！」接著平板又開始播放影片了。

是一個穿著藍花衣裳的太太，她一出現少年就驚喊：「這個好像我外婆哦！」

And indeed she was Wendi's grandma. She was following a schoolgirl with braided pigtails who was supposedly Wendi's mother. She hadn't noticed anyone following her and went into a bakery shop. "Hi, what are your two-for-one specials today?" To her question, the shop proprietor replied, "Today we have the cornbread and croissant. How about one of each?" He and the girl were acquaintances.

She nodded her head in an emphatic yes. After having paid for the bread, she thanked the owner heartily and left with her pigtails bouncing up and down as she happily trotted back home.

After the schoolgirl had left, the woman went into the shop and greeted the owner, "Thanks, Lee." The proprietor replied, "Don't mention it. Those bread would be on sale before closing anyway. Your daughter is amazing in how she wants to help people." The woman smiled, "Thanks for all your help." Pointing in the direction of the schoolgirl, she continued, "She doesn't know our arrangement. Please keep this a secret." The owner nodded and smiled as they waved each other good-bye.

The schoolgirl hid the bread under her clothes as she was about to go into the house. After making sure no one was home, she quickly went to her room and hid the bread in her

花衣裳太太就是少年的外婆，她走在路上跟著前面一個麻花辮子小女學生，看來應該是少年的媽媽學生時的樣子，她沒發現後面有個人偷偷跟著她，走進了一家麵包店，堆著笑容問了老闆一聲：「老闆，今天買一送一的麵包有什麼？」老闆應該是熟人，回答女學生說：「今天有玉米的和牛角麵包，各一個好不好啊？」

　　她聽了以後用力點點頭，掏出錢來給老闆換了麵包，大大地謝謝老闆就走出店門了。買了兩個麵包的小女學生就跳著走回家去，小腦勺後的兩條麻花辮子隨著她開心地飛著。

　　等女學生一走，花衣太太進了麵包店。「老李，謝謝你呀！」老李回答她：「客氣什麼！本來就打烊的特價，你女兒這個好，能幫助人不得了啊。」花衣太太也笑著說：「還得靠您幫忙！」手邊指著小女學生離開的方向邊再交代老闆：「她不知道，您得幫我保密啊！」老闆笑著點頭道好，太太就揮手向他告辭。

　　小女學生到家門口了還把兩小麵包塞進衣服裡藏著，看了看家裡，見沒人了才快步走進去躲回房間，將衣服裡的麵包迅速地放進書包裡。

school bag.

The next day, with her school uniform already on, the girl set off for school early with the two pieces of bread and the breakfast that her mother had prepared for her. When she was near the school entrance, another girl with the same braided pigtails was waiting for her. The two of them appeared to be classmates. The latter looked quite shy, but she had an expectant look in her eyes.

The schoolgirl told her, "My mom made me this huge rice ball today, and I saw her put an egg in it, too. It's going to taste great. Come. Let's go in." The girls walked hand in hand into their classroom.

In the classroom, she took out the rice ball and the two pieces of bread from yesterday, the sight of which was enough to make them giggle in joy. The girl used a spoon to divide everything up neatly in half, and they shared the food contentedly.

While eating, the schoolgirl said, "Didn't you tell me you had almost used up your pencil and eraser? I remember I still have the new pencil and eraser that I won from my last essay competition. You can have them because my pencil is still good. You can sign up for the next competition, and then

隔天一早，小女學生穿戴整齊準備上學去，揣著昨天買的兩個麵包和媽媽幫她準備的早餐在書包裡早早上學去了。到了校門口，另一個小麻花辮正等著她，應該是她同班同學，明顯覷腆得多，不過一雙眼睛明亮亮地露著渴望。

　　女學生拉著小麻花辮説：「今天我媽幫我捏了一個大飯糰，我還看到她加了滷蛋，一定很好吃！走，快進教室。」兩人手牽手欣喜地進校門。

　　到教室裡，小女學生拿出大飯糰和昨天那兩個小麵包，就這麼點東西把她倆看得笑開懷，女學生用湯匙柄將每一個都分成一半，和小麻花辮開心地吃了起來。

　　女學生邊吃著邊説：「你上次不是説鉛筆和橡皮擦都禿了嗎？我想起上次作文比賽佳作送的獎品還有鉛筆和橡皮擦，送給你，我的鉛筆還很長，下次如果有什麼比賽，你去跟老師報名，這樣就不怕沒文具了！」小麻花辮心裡開花了，本來因為家裡窮，也沒人幫她張羅生活，買不起文具還吃不上飽飯，連學費都是爸媽借來的，

you won't have to worry about not having a pencil or eraser anymore." The little girl was thrilled to hear that. She came from a poor family and had little money for school supplies or food. Her father even had to borrow money to pay her tuition. It was wonderful of her classmate to share food and school stationery with her and show her ways to get free school supplies. There is always a solution to a problem. She nodded happily in agreement as she chowed down the food.

These two girls were growing up in so much love from all the people quietly looking after them.

The next video clip showed a middle-aged woman doing her house chores while watching TV. To Wendi, the woman in the video seemed at once both familiar and distant even though she was his own mother.

A TV commercial caught her eye. "Lack of school funding in this remote village…teachers trying to raise tuition money for kids…" She continued with the housework but stopped suddenly as she thought of something.

She walked over to her purse on the dining room table and took out an envelope of money. She counted out a few bills and set them aside. She then counted out some more and put them in her purse and put some bills back in the envelope, which left

以為往後真的要沒鉛筆寫功課了，還好有這位好同學，不僅送她文具，和她分食，還教她想辦法，原來事情可以這麼解決，開心地邊吃邊向同伴點頭同意。

　　畫面裡倆小女生吃著幾個大人默默的愛心，繼續她們長大的每一天。

　　接下來畫面快轉到一個中年婦女正在做家事，家裡面電視陪著她說話。少年看到自己媽媽，有點熟悉又有點陌生的感覺。

　　一個廣告吸引她抬起頭看了幾眼：「偏鄉弱勢學童家中的教育資源不足……偏鄉老師要替學生的學費發愁……」把廣告看完後，她繼續原來的工作，幾秒後又想到了什麼而停了下來。

　　放下手邊的工作走到客廳桌上拿出包包裡的一包錢，把手上一把錢數了幾張放在一邊，再數幾張放回包包，再數幾張放回信封，剩一張千元大鈔，她慢慢地放在旁邊電話櫃上用便條紙盒壓著。

her with just a single 1,000-dollar bill that she slowly put under a memo pad by the telephone.

That sight prompted Wendi to softly exclaim, "Only 1,000 dollars (about US$33) this month for my allowance?"

The boy's mother was caught up in her thought as she took out another 1,000-dollar bill from her purse, intending to put it by the telephone. She looked at the TV and thought again and again about where she should put the bill. Eventually, she put it right next to the telephone.

"So there's your NT$2,000 allowance," Data said.

"I've never had 2,000 dollars before. It's usually $1,500. Was that for this month?" Wendi was confused.

A boy now appeared in the video. He saw the $1,500 by the telephone, picked it up, and turned around and said to his mother, "Mom, what about the money for my new shoes?" The question reminded the boy of a conversation that he had had with his mother a few months before.

With a little difficulty, his mother replied, "Your shoes should last a few more months. Let's talk about it later. Or you can try to save some money on your own for the shoes. I don't have more to give you this month."

Mad, the boy said, "There's almost a hole in the front of my

少年看到，小聲喊著：「這個月零用錢才一千塊？」

少年的媽媽停在那裡想了想，走過去從包裡抽回一千塊，想添到電話櫃上，又再看著電視，想了又想，想了再想，還是把一千塊放到了電話邊。

「你的兩千塊零用錢原來是這麼來的。」庫哥說。

「我沒拿過兩千塊……通常都是一千五，這是這個月的嗎？」少年也疑惑。

再後來畫面中少年出現了，看到電話旁的一千五百塊錢，就拿著回頭問他媽媽：「媽，那我買鞋的錢呢？」畫面裡的少年這麼說著，畫面外的少年想起來前幾個月和媽媽有這麼一段。

媽媽為難地回答他：「你鞋還可以再穿幾個月，以後再買，不然你省點花，看看能不能自己想辦法存錢買嘛，媽媽這個月沒多的錢了。」

少年生氣地說：「鞋前面都快磨破了，如果破掉了

shoe. What if people see my toes? I'm not going to look good in them."

Now the mother was getting mad, too. "We'll deal with it then if that happens next month. Do you know how lucky you are to even have an allowance? Some kids don't even have money for food. Let's see how good you'll look when you have no money."

"Well, I already don't have any money, so we don't need to wait till that day. Forget it! This is how it always is every time we talk about this. Just forget we even talked." With that, the boy stormed out of the house.

The video ended.

The boy said, "Did my mother give away my shoe money to the charity?" Data answered, "No, she couldn't even do that. She took $500 from grocery money to add to the $1,000 for your allowance."

"But wasn't she gonna give money to that charity on TV? Why didn't she?" The boy questioned.

"She wanted to, but the following month she had to save more money for your allowance and new shoes. Therefore, she still wasn't able to give," Data said as he looked at the boy's new shoes.

還穿多沒面子啊！」

　　媽媽聽了也生氣地回嗆少年：「下個月如果破掉再買嘛，你能上學還有零用錢已經很幸福了知不知道？有的小孩還沒飯吃呢！每天面子面子的，等哪天你沒錢花我看你那面子還能幹嘛？」

　　「我已經沒錢花了，不用等哪天。算了！每次跟你說這個你都要說一堆，不講了。」說完少年就出門去了。

　　畫面收起。

　　看完這段，少年說：「我媽是不是把買鞋的錢捐出去了？」

　　庫哥回答他：「沒有，她連捐的錢都沒有，那個月是從家裡花用的買菜錢裡節出五百塊為了湊到你的一千五百塊零用錢。」

　　「可是她不是很想捐那個電視說的嗎？怎麼最後沒捐？」少年懷疑道

　　「她本來想捐的，但是再下個月，她又從買菜錢裡湊了你的零用錢和現在腳上的新鞋。」庫哥看了看少年的鞋，再看看他。「所以還是沒有錢捐。」

Wendi also looked at his new shoes and remembered that he had complained to his mother how ugly the new shoes were when he first saw them.

Data smiled and said to Wendi, "Your mother is a good person. She still wanted to give even though she didn't have very much money."

The boy was now deep in thought as he gazed at the river. After a while, he said, "So giving is good?"

"Well, maybe. Why don't you give it a try?" Data was game. "But if you do it for her, it may not be that satisfying. I'd venture to say that money was not really the point. The point is how she was touched and inspired when she saw people who needed help. Besides, you don't have the money anyway because you're still in school. Why don't you save up your allowances like how she saved up hers? You two can find a worthy project to support like an orphanage, free lunches for seniors, or scholarships. This will help her fulfill her wishes and feel useful even when she is sick. Without a doubt, this will make her happy."

The boy was still unsure. "Will it be too late to start saving money now?"

Laughing, Data said, "If you don't start now, everything that

少年順著他的眼才看到自己的鞋，回想起那時看到新鞋還向他媽媽抱怨鞋子有點醜的事。

　　庫哥微笑地看著少年説：「你媽媽人還真是不錯，明明自己沒有很多錢，還是想幫助別人。」

　　看完少年若有所思地望著河邊，久久後才説：「所以是捐錢嗎？」

　　「或許有用。試試看不就知道了？」庫哥真有實驗精神。「但我覺得你幫她捐會很無感，其實我猜捐錢不是重點，是她看到了有人需要幫助就想出點力吧。而且你是學生也沒那麼多閒錢，不如你學她把你的零用錢存起來，和她一起找需要幫助的對象，例如育幼院還是獨居老人共餐或助學金什麼的，也讓她感覺自己就算生病，也還是能幫助人，既滿足了她之前的心願又讓她覺得自己有用，那就不是或許了，肯定會快樂。」

　　少年將信將疑地説：「從現在開始存錢，來不來得及啊？」

　　庫哥哈哈的笑了。「就怕你連開始都沒有，那我們

we talked about today will be for nothing, and you'll just go right back to worrying about her like before." Data continued, "It seems you wish to pay back the kindness you were given. Let's see what the tablet says about the value system we should have."

The tablet displayed the word, "Gratitude."

Make genuine efforts to show gratitude to your family, your community, and Mother Nature.

All successful people remember the kindness they received and try to pay it back as a matter of course. Grateful people constantly receive more blessings, and the doors keep opening up for them.

If your parents are still alive, please cherish their presence. If you wish to do anything for them, do so ASAP. Waiting may leave you sorry for the rest of your life.

Once Tzu Chi sponsored a year-end blessing ceremony at a prison. One of the inmates had never had even one visitor in three years. Without his knowledge, Tzu Chi quietly invited that inmates' family members to attend. At the event, with tears rolling down his cheek, he confided to the volunteers that he missed his father the most. Suddenly, his father and his two children appeared right in front of him. He was in total shock,

今天就白忙了，你還是繼續煩惱你媽媽的病吧。」接著又說：「你想起對你有恩的人，想要回報。我們來看平板怎麼說，該儲值什麼樣的信念吧？」

緊接，平板出現了「感恩心」：

學會對家人報恩，對社會感恩，對大自然感恩。

知恩圖報，成功的人都是知恩不忘本，那才是理所當然。因為他們體悟到懂得感恩的人，獲得的越來越多，路會越走越寬。

因為感受到溫暖，感受到自己有價值，而變得更好，所以也想做些好事，來證明施恩於我的人與自己的努力沒有白費，回饋更是肯定自己有社會價值的方法。

如果你的父母還健在，請好好的珍惜，千萬不要留下遺憾。因為錯過了，一定會後悔而遺憾終生。

某監獄於歲末舉辦祝福活動，志工悄悄邀請一位受刑三年未曾有人探視的同學家人出席活動，但沒事先告訴同學，打算給他一個驚喜。志工詢問受刑同學心情，

and immediately knelt down and wept bitterly. He hugged his father and repented, "Dad, I'm sorry. I'm sorry." Hugging his father tightly, it seemed as if he would never let him go, and the sadness of it all moved everyone to tears. The inmate said he had failed to take care of his children and his parents, and he promised his father that he would be like a reborn man after his release from prison. "Dad, I'll be a good son to you. Please wait for me. I will take good care of my kids, too. I won't make you sad again," said the inmate. His father, in his 80s, said, "I will wait for you. You take good care of yourself." The inmate could not stop crying from the moment he saw his father and kids. At first, his father had not really wanted to attend the ceremony at the prison. His father had only agreed to attend after volunteers' repeated invitations. As the inmate just had his birthday, their surprise visit was like the best gift he'd ever had. He still had 17 more years remaining on his sentence, and he was not sure if he would ever see his father again. His poignancy was palpable which would haunt everyone who was there at the ceremony long after that day.

Acts of filial piety need to be delivered at a speed greater than that of aging or untimely death of our parents. Do not say, "I will do it when I have time." The present is the future that

同學表示最想念父親，說時還淚流滿頰。突然父親和一雙兒女出現在他面前時，他一臉驚訝不敢置信，馬上跪地，痛哭流涕，抱住父親懺悔道：「爸爸，我對不起您！我對不起您！」緊緊抱住父親，久久不願放手，現場所有人無不紅了眼眶，頻頻拭淚。受刑同學說，以前對兒女未盡父責，對父母未盡孝道，他向父親保證，出獄後會重新生活：「爸爸，我會好好孝順您，您要等我回來，我會好好照顧孩子，不會再讓您傷心了。」因志工三番兩次邀約，才勉強成行的八十餘歲父親終於開口：「我會等你回來，你在這裡要加油！」同學從見到父親與兒女之後，眼淚就沒停過，他的生日剛過，能夠見到日夜想念的親人，是他有生以來最好的禮物了。但他還有十七年的刑期，還不知等不等得到可以親自奉養老父，看到這一幕，忍不住的惆悵縈繞心頭，讓人低迴不已。

　　孝順的速度要大於父母老化或意外的速度，不要

has arrived from the past. If you didn't do it in the past and you still won't do it in the present, then you may not get an opportunity to do it in the future.

"You're right. It's better late than never." The boy was reminded how helpless he had felt earlier that day. "But if she gives me a hard time again, then I'll remind her about the time when she spent her allowance on the bread when she was a schoolgirl."

Suddenly feeling confident, the boy stood up as if he were about to embark on an important mission. He then waved good-bye to Data and left.

Data muttered to himself, "Maybe it wasn't such a bad thing that your mother got sick. You seemed to have gotten something good out of it. Not bad.

拿「等以後有時間」當藉口，現在就是過去的未來，以前不去做、現在不馬上去做、未來也不一定有機會做了。

「也對，現在及時出招總比沒招好。」少年不想回到之前那種無助的情緒裡。「如果她又罵我……」少年又猶豫了一下。「那我就嗆她小時候拿零用錢去買麵包的事！」

少年忽然間底氣十足，站起來像是要去幹什麼大事業一樣和庫哥揮手道別。

庫哥看著少年離開的背影，喃喃道：「想想你媽媽的病來得也不算壞，讓你知道些事情，或是讓你改變點什麼，好像也不錯。」

第六章
CHAPTER 6

我不知道你，你也不知道我，
愛著你
Loving Each Other and
Not Knowing It

Sitting on the riverbank, the boy brought Data up to date on how the donation thing had gone with his mother. Right after he handed her three hundred dollars and a donation form, she kept looking at him curiously, making him blush. He was quite self-conscious yet excited as this was the first time he had given anything to a worthy cause. His face was red from all the excitement. His mother kept crying and praising Wendi and saying that he's finally grown up. She was extremely happy that he had shown love toward other people. What's more surprising to the mother was how he had learned that she had wanted to make donations, but Wendi would not divulge his source. He would not talk about Data except to say that he had come across those people who could use some help.

For a few days afterward, the boy seemed to be living his best life. The way his mom looked at him completely changed, almost like how a fan would look at a celebrity. He felt as if he was floating on cloud nine. On top of that, his mom had been more lenient toward him and his school work as long as he kept out of trouble. She had also been making his favorite foods for him more often.

With less allowance each month, he wasn't able to buy drinks or go out whenever and wherever he wanted.

這天庫哥和少年在河堤邊聊著上回說要和媽媽商量捐款的事，一開始少年遞給媽媽一張捐款表和三百塊，媽媽狐疑地看著他，少年羞赧地不敢直視媽媽的眼睛，對於自己第一次有意義的善行害羞地無法自處，跟庫哥說起時還是超不好意思的滿臉通紅，但一臉的興奮和庫哥報告當他拿出那張捐款表時，媽媽哭著誇他長大了，很高興看到他這麼有愛心，而且竟然知道媽媽心裡想著這件事，問他怎麼知道的，少年就是絕口不提庫哥，只說是偶然看到這些人需要幫助。

　　此後，他過了生平以來自認為最快樂的幾天，每天媽媽看他的眼光都不一樣了，那眼神好像在看街口那個很會讀書出了名的大哥哥一樣，心都要飄上天了。

　　少年心情爽朗，好像轉移注意力到幫助別人這件事以後，媽媽比較少挑剔他的學校表現，自己只要在學校不惹麻煩，每天上學心情沒像之前一樣「壓力山大」。

　　而且媽媽比以往更常煮一些好吃的給他吃，少年自覺這個改變太好了！

　　雖然每個月少了零用錢，不能買飲料，不能想去哪就去哪。還好他本來就沒那種喜歡帶他去花大錢的朋

Fortunately, he didn't have friends who were big spenders anyway. Now, whenever he wanted to buy things, the boy would touch the money in his pocket and tell himself the money had already been spoken for. Comparing what he was going to spend the money on to what the money could do for the students who had no money to pay for school, it was an easy decision.

Thank goodness for Data; otherwise, Wendi probably never would have come up with that idea and certainly would not have changed.

He had never thought about anyone else besides himself. After seeing his mother as a young girl and the things she had done, the boy came to realize that not everything is what it seemed. Perhaps the truth was hiding somewhere he didn't look.

That made him think of someone.

"Data, if you were able to find my mother and grandma, then…how about my father?" The boy's mind just wouldn't rest.

"I guess so. Let me try. You're thinking about your pop?"

"We'd never spent any time together. I wouldn't know what it'd be like to have a father," the boy said after some thought.

友。每次像之前一樣要花錢時，掏一掏口袋想到自己錢拿去別的地方用了，就不自覺的把手收回來，一想到自己以往把同一把錢拿去花在這些東西上面，和捐出去幫其他學生繳學費相比，後者比較重要，他其實很願意做這個決定。

真是幸好有庫哥，不然自己想不出這種招數，也不可能作這種嘗試。

少年從沒像現在一樣感受到自己的生命裡其實還活著別人，看見小時候的媽媽，看見媽媽在自己背後的一些事，他領悟到很多事不是自以為的那樣，也許在自己看不到的地方才藏著真相。

於是少年想到一個人。

「庫哥，你可以在資料中找到媽媽和外婆，那……也可以找到我爸嗎？」果然，少年又出招了。

「可以吧，找找看，你想看你爸？」

「我沒和我爸相處過，我不知道有爸爸是什麼感覺。」少年深思，「小時候我想到他會生氣，也想過如果我爸還在該有多好，但長大後就沒感覺了。」

"When I was little, I used to get angry thinking about him, but I would also fantasize how life would be with a father. But as I grew older, I just didn't think about him anymore."

"I'm not sure how it would feel to have a father. A small kid probably doesn't feel much, but then as the kid gets bigger, it must be a special feeling for the dad…like a duplicate of himself suddenly standing in front of him, and there is no denying that he made this person, whether he liked it or not." Data was totally immersed in his own make-believe role.

The boy waited for Data to finish his monologue before asking, "How's it you can feel so much for one who's never had a father?"

"Those were not my sentiments. I got all of them from the internet. Thank you." Data quipped with a fake smile.

"So, can we get on with my problem now?" Wendi was trying to laugh but seemed visibly impatient.

"Young people are always so impatient," Data mumbled as he took out his tablet and went to work. Wendi was not amused.

Data pulled out a timeline from the screen, zoomed in on a section labeled with the name of the boy's mom.

"I wanted to see my dad, not my mom, duh," the boy reminded Data.

「我也不知道有爸爸是什麼感覺。但我覺得小時候還蠻可以的，長大了爸爸這角色在兒子身上很……特別，好像複製人的概念：一個和自己形象一樣的人忽然長出來，然後還是自己生產的，想不想承認都矛盾。」庫哥很能融入情境，自己演起來了。

　　少年等著他演完開了岔的思路說：「你怎麼沒爸爸還那麼多感慨啊？」

　　「網路文字脈絡分析的結果，作者不是我，謝謝。」庫哥一本正經地回答少年。

　　「那可以繼續我的問題了嗎？」少年面露假笑地提醒他。

　　「青少年就心急，真難聊天……」庫哥邊抱怨邊拿出平板和曾被嫌慢的十根手指來工作，少年臉上頓時三條線。

　　庫哥在平板面上拉出一條時間軸，把其中一段放大，少年看上面寫著媽媽的名字說，「我是要看我爸，這是我媽……」

"I know, but there doesn't seem to be enough information on your father. I'm going through your mom's memories to find him." Data explained to the boy.

"What are you, Sherlock?" Wendi said with a snap. He didn't know what he was feeling; it was as if everything he'd experienced was in his brain, but he just couldn't retrieve those memories. Wendi also didn't want to be vulnerable—he didn't want to show how anxious he felt at this moment.

After working for a while, Data handed the tablet to the boy.

On the screen, a gaunt young man was shown holding a photo of an infant. "Wendi..." the man said quietly, his eyes filled with guilt and shame.

Data glanced over at the boy. Seeing his father, a whole human being, before him for the first time brought tears to Wendi's eyes.

「我還不知道你爸是誰，還得交叉比對你媽的記憶時間點才能找到片段，資料好像不太夠，我再比對關係人物找找看。」庫哥劈里啪啦地邊說邊操作著平板，完全沒閒著。

「你在當柯南嗎？」少年眼看自己又被徵信了一次，心情好複雜，把自己過去什麼好的壞的作為攤在別人面前，就算自己或許知道或許不想記起，但什麼過往都像在時間河裡泡著，沒浮上水面以為看不到，其實都在，而且還改變不了，心裡果然忐忑。但要他從現在開始不耍酷、不擺爛、不犯傻，又好像很沒把握，什麼時候自己沒注意，又原形畢露了，真傷腦筋。

庫哥忙活了一會兒，把平板拿給少年看。

「文諦……」畫面裡一個瘦瘦的年輕男子看著相本裡一張嬰兒照說話，但只說了一句又停了許久，欲言又止的表情裡，眼神流出了慚愧。

庫哥側過臉觀察楞住的某少年，這位看到自己印象不深刻的爸爸清清楚楚地、有動作帶表情地呈現在自己眼前，情緒一時激動，什麼話都沒說，眼眶先紅了。

The man on the screen put down the photo and began to write a letter.

Dearest Wendi,

Dad didn't abandon you. I wanted to keep you, but you were still so young. I thought it best to leave you with your mom because I know how horrible it is to grow up without a mother. I was such a child. When you're older, I'll discuss with your mom to have you live with me. I can't wait to take you to amusement parks, fly kites in parks, watch baseball games, and much, much more. Are you mad at me, Wendi? It was my fault that your mom and I got divorced. Dad didn't want to leave you. I didn't want to live without you, your hugs, your laughter, your calling me "Dad".

By the time he read to this point, he had had to take a couple of deep breaths just to hold back his tears. The man on the screen continued writing.

Wendi is all grown up now. I heard that despite falling quite a few times on your bike, you've learned how to ride it. It's such a shame that I can't witness in person how great you

畫面中男子把相本放下，開始在信紙上寫字：

「文諦，爸爸沒有不要你，我是想把你留在我這裡
的，但是你還太小，一定需要比較多媽媽的照顧。爸爸
太清楚沒有媽媽的小孩有多可憐，因為爸爸就是這樣長
大的，我不想讓你和我一樣苦，等你長大一點，我再跟
媽媽商量讓你和爸爸住。爸爸想帶你去遊樂園玩，想和
你一起放風箏、看球賽，好多好多。文諦會不會怪爸爸？
是爸爸做錯事，所以才和媽媽離婚，爸爸很不想跟你分
開，但只能先忍耐你不在身邊，不能抱你，不能看到你
笑，不能聽你叫爸爸……」

少年看到這裡，已經忍不住深呼吸好幾口氣，才不
至於讓眼框裡的淚水潰堤。而畫面裡的男子依然故我地
寫著信。

「文諦是小男子漢，聽說你會騎腳踏車了，不過摔
了好幾個破皮，呵呵，好可惜爸爸沒看到你厲害的樣子，
不然爸爸一定幫你大大的鼓掌。」

look on a bike, but best believe I am cheering you on!

The man sealed the letter, placed it between the pages of a book, took a deep breath, and wiped away his tears as the screen faded to black.

Suddenly, the next image on the screen showed a man covered in blood being transported onto an ambulance as paramedics performed CPR on him.

"Dad!" the boy gasped as he saw the scene. At this moment, as the man's heart was starting to beat again, the paramedics quickly put the oxygen mask on him. The man opened his mouth. The paramedics got closer to the man and Wendi got closer to the tablet in the hope of hearing him better. Data zoomed in to the man's mouth, and Wendi saw and heard:

"Wendi...I'm sorry...Dad is sorry...Wendi..." For every word the man spoke, a tear came rolling down his cheeks. With this, a machine let out a long, monotonous beep, prompting the medics to continue trying to save him as the screen turned black again.

For a long, long time, the boy sat still on the grass, quietly staring blankly at the black screen. He kept thinking, "Those were Dad's last words? How did I not know how much he loved

男子收起信紙折好放在一本書裡夾著，深吸了一口氣後用手抹抹眼淚後，畫面就黑了。

下一秒畫面跳到一個滿臉是血的男子身上，少年有點擔心地看著畫面裡的爸爸昏迷不醒，被人用擔架抬上救護車，旁邊的醫護人員緊急地幫他做心肺復甦術。

「爸！」少年輕呼了一聲。畫面裡的爸爸剛好在這時救回了一點心跳，醫護人員不敢鬆懈，趕緊幫他掛上氧氣面罩，這時男子嘴巴動了幾下，醫護人員貼近耳朵想聽清楚，平板外的少年也著急地想聽清楚，也把耳朵貼了過去，庫哥連忙幫他把畫面對焦在男子嘴上放大，少年急著看，也聽到了：

「文諦，爸爸對不起……對不起……對不起……文諦……」男子每說一次對不起，就流下一滴眼淚。

才說完，心跳監測儀就發出長嗶聲，男子再度失去心跳，旁邊的醫護人員又忙了起來。

漸漸地畫面也暗了下來。

好久好久，少年靜止在原本姿勢，坐在草皮上盯著平板，表情凝肅，腦子裡止不住地回放著各種問題：

me? And I was mad at him this whole time. He didn't get the happy ending he'd hoped for, and he died so unhappy. How can I still be mad at him? And where's that letter he had written? How come I never got it? Did he not mail it in time? There are so many things in life that don't arrive in time."

The boy kept thinking and thinking, but endless questions just kept popping out on his mind. After Wendi had settled down a little, Data said slowly, "Seems like you and your dad have some unfinished business. Your longing for him and his love for you have always been there—the message just never got through because there was not a messenger."

Wendi took a deep, slow breath in through his nose, out his mouth, but he still couldn't get words out of his mouth. Data was relieved to see the boy move; he was scared that Wendi might end up not breathing like his dad.

At this point, the boy felt an urge to do something. He had a lot to say but couldn't get them off his chest, so he stood up and headed straight for the riverbank.

Facing the water, the boy yelled, "Dad, it's okay. I'm not mad at you anymore, so don't you be sad. You're my only dad. Please accept me as your son again. Please rest in peace." Suddenly, Wendi began sobbing, "Can...can we...can we..."

「這就是爸爸生命結束前最後的話嗎？

「他這麼掛念我？我卻什麼都不知道，也氣了他好幾年。他以為的「以後」並沒有出現，他一樣也很難過，這樣，算是含恨而終吧！再氣他好像也有點殘忍⋯⋯

那封信呢？我怎麼從來沒收到過？是來不及寄？人生有好多個來不及啊！」

少年心裡越想越多，一個個的問題不斷冒出。

庫哥讓少年先沉澱一下才開口，慢慢地說：「看來你們父子之間的信息沒有搭上，你有對他的想念，他有對你的愛，都是存在的，不過沒人幫忙送信。」

少年深吸了一口氣再慢慢吐了出來，之後還是說不出話來。不過還好有動靜了，不然庫哥都要以為他跟著他爸爸一起忘了呼吸。

現在少年滿身的衝動想做點什麼，心口好像有滿腔的話想說但吐不出來，於是站起來急切地走向河邊。

少年對著河邊喊：「爸，沒關係，我不氣了你，你不要難過，你是我唯一的爸爸，請你重新接受我這個兒子，現在你可以安息了。」說著說著就哭了起來，「我們⋯⋯我們以後⋯⋯我們以後⋯⋯」少年實在泣不成

The boy couldn't get the words out his mouth, "Dad…"

The boy didn't realize how much he missed his father, how he wished he were right there next to him, riding bikes together, playing sports together. He wanted it all.

Witnessing this, Data let the boy be. He needed to let it all out. "How nice it must be to have a dad who loves you…I mean, look at me."

"I'm so relieved," Wendi said. "All this time I thought my dad had left because he didn't want me. Now I understand, and I need to tell my mom."

"What if she asks you how you knew? What would you say?" Data asked.

Suddenly it dawned on the boy that he could never bring up his business with Data under any circumstances unless he wants people to think he has gone mad.

Data was like a best-kept secret that Wendi got to keep all to himself and no one else, and that had created no small amount of pressure on the boy.

"I said you need to think about me. You never thought about me not having a father. Do you care how I feel?"

"But you're a computer program. Are you supposed to even have feelings?"

聲，「爸……」原來自己有這麼想念爸爸，想要爸爸在身邊，想要爸爸真的和他一起去騎腳踏車、一起去打球，都想，什麼都想。

庫哥看著少年對父親的不捨，知道他需要時間消化才得回來的父愛，就讓他流一會兒淚吧。

「真好，有爸爸愛你耶，『你要想想我』。」庫哥用彆腳方法幫少年打氣。

「忽然覺得好開心，我爸不是因為討厭我才離開我們，我能理解他，我也要回去跟我媽講。」

「她若問你怎麼知道的，你怎麼回答？」庫哥反問少年。

少年恍然醒覺，庫哥的事不知道該如何向第三人提起，或是連提都不該提，否則別人要把他當精神病了。

「庫哥」這個祕密像是個不能公開的大禮物一樣，只能自己嗨，不能一起嗨。把這種禮物揣在懷裡的心理壓力還真不是天般的大……

「我說你要想想我！你都沒想到我沒有爸爸！你有考慮過我的感受嗎？」

「你是電腦人，你該有感受嗎？」

"It's exactly because I don't have feelings that I know how empty and unattached I am. I have tons of knowledge but no emotions or memories of any event to speak of." Data gave itself a cold and sensible assessment worthy of a computer program. "All right now, let's watch a story." Data opened up his tablet and it displayed, "Believe in Love."

A young drug addict at a detention center said self-righteously, "I never had a father, and my mother remarried. I'm a forgotten kid. No one wants me; no one cares what I think. There'll be no one crying when I'm gone. Drugs are the only thing that'll help me forget the future." However, when his uncle showed him a letter from his father written just before he died, the kid had a catharsis as he realized how much his father had loved him. He was able to open up and believe that there is still love in the world. Only love can transcend a person.

We are predestined to meet certain people and never cross paths with others. Maybe this is called karma. It is especially true when it comes to kinship, in which there are no absolute rights or wrongs, only sorrows and griefs that the children cannot forget and forgive. There are things that they may never understand why their parents did at the time. Time heals many things, but not the lasting legacies of parental trauma. The

「我就是沒感受所以更反思出自己很空洞，只有知識、只剩理性，但不附著於任何一段生命歷程。」庫哥剖析自己也是理性有餘、冷酷無情，不負自己電腦人名號。「好啦，我們來看個故事吧！」庫哥説著打開平板，顯示「儲值相信愛」——

在觀護所裡有個犯毒品案的青少年，他很理直氣壯地説，我從小就沒有父親，母親又再婚，我是被遺棄的孩子，沒有人想要了解我，即使我不在了，也不會有人感到悲傷，我只能藉毒品來讓自己忘掉未來。

可是當他的伯父找到他父親的遺書，向他述説父親遺書中字裡行間所傳達的愛，他痛哭流涕地釋懷了。他終於打開心門，相信人間有愛，唯有相信愛，才能遇見更好的自己。

人的一生中，你肯定會遇見了誰，也肯定會錯過了誰，也許那是冥冥之中早已註定的緣分。尤其親情的愛，沒有對錯，也沒有所謂的是非，只有那個還有遺憾、還有抱怨的自己，因他們的苦，孩子們也無法理解，時間雖會沖淡一切，只有牽掛，沖淡不了。當心情不好的時候，總是會將責任歸咎於身邊的人或環境。

instinct is to blame people or circumstances when bad things happen.

The 2020 coronavirus pandemic is a sober reminder of our relationship with nature. Besides boosting our immune system, a spiritual cleansing is also in order so as to live well in this pandemic. Was this a Darwinian survival-of-the-fittest event? Will our religious beliefs take us where we want to go? Apparently, instead of living a predestined life, our fate is largely determined by our thoughts and actions. If a person truly believes without a shadow of a doubt that certain things will happen to him, whether right or wrong, good or bad, chances are they will surely happen to him. During the lockdown, some people set up a schedule for themselves reading books or taking online classes, a sort of spiritual cultivation and cleansing, while others chose to squander away their days on sleeping, playing mindless games, or binge-watching movies, essentially suffocating their minds. Evidently, an eco-friendly life is about supplanting harmful beliefs with virtuous thoughts, which in themselves require merit and are a blessing.

Change your ways. Believe in love. The invisible force of the universe will support you like a mountain, watching over you

像二〇二〇上半年肆虐全球的新冠肺炎，再次牽引人們思索自身與環境的連結：除了強健身體提升免疫力，還要倡議心靈上的環保，這場天災，會否是一個物競天擇的過程？是否，你信仰什麼，你的生命就會往那個方向走？人的命運顯然並非由上天註定，而是取決於人的思想與行動，如果真正深信某件事會發生，則不管這件事是善是惡、是好是壞，這件事就一定會發生在這個人身上。疫情盛行期，許多人居家檢疫或隔離，同樣被關在家裡，有人選擇讀書、線上學習，生活規律自律，這不僅是勤耕智慧田，更是在心靈上做環保；反觀有人則是成天睡覺、追劇、玩遊戲，渾渾噩噩地度過每一天，這無疑是在心靈上囤積拉垃。由此觀之，用好的信念，清理不好的信念，是心靈環保的原則。有好的信念是一種福，想給自己種福，就必須建立好的信念。

　　當你轉過身時，相信有愛，就可以讓背後的人用雙手來支持你的背，像背後一座大山，感受這股無形支持的力量，看著你的未來，走向你的未來。

as you embark on your future.

In an effort to soothe the boy, Data did a few somersaults and traded a few punches with him for fun. Finally, Wendi calmed down, and it was time to bid each other good-bye as they had no excuse to stay any later than they already had.

The boy went home with the warmth and fullness of his father's love in his heart. His strides seemed quicker and lighter, and a thought suddenly occurred to him. In the past, he felt lost like floating duckweeds, but now he had found his roots, which would serve him well as he continued to grow and thrive like a tree that would grow big and tall.

為平撫少年情緒，庫哥突地翻了幾下跟斗，並和少年打打鬧鬧，總算平緩了少年激動的心情，稍微回復正常後也必須向彼此說 bye bye，時間很晚，再不回家就很難為晚歸找藉口了。

　　少年今天收獲滿滿，把滿肚子的「爸爸愛我」帶回家，走起路來輕鬆多了。他忽然有種感覺，自己以前像個浮萍一樣，今天忽然成了小樹長出根來扎到了地下，等哪天也能長成頂天立地的大樹一般。

第七章
CHAPTER 7

有問題？沒問題！
The Metamorphosis

As soon as he got to the riverbank near the grass field, the boy saw a familiar figure by the bushes and shouted excitedly, "Hey, there you are, earlier than usual. I guess you can't wait to see me."

"What if I tell you this is the last time we'll ever see each other?"

"Is this another test? You told me last time that life is like a battery that starts out with a full charge and then slowly drains bit by bit. That's why it's important to find meaningful things to do while we still have the charge."

Data said, "That's right, and now our battery is almost running empty. Ask me anything now. Although I disguised myself with an algorithm, it can still be cracked in just a few minutes. That's when I'll have to be on my way."

"Is there an assassin going after you? I didn't know people also play hooky in the Cloud." The boy was surprised.

"Playing hooky? Is that like a serious job here?" Data rolled his eyes.

"OK. Enough. Here. Take this tablet." Data handed the boy his tablet and gave him instructions on how to use the computer such as where to turn it on and charge the battery.

少年這天走到河堤邊的草坡就看到灌木叢旁熟悉的人，開心的喊著：「哈！今天你比我還迫不及待見面啊！反常哦～」戲謔的微笑掛在少年嘴角。

　　「如果我跟你說這次將是我們最後一次見面了，你會如何？」

　　「又要考我？你上次說人生就和電池一樣，一充好就是等著被用完，所以要把握有電的時候找到自己要的東西。」

　　「對，現在就是那個快沒電的時候了，你想問什麼就問吧，我放了個偽裝程式在外頭，破解只要幾分鐘，完了我就該『跑路』了。」

　　「你被追殺啦？想不到電腦人的世界也有跑路這行業……」少年驚奇道。

　　「跑路在你們這裡算是一種行業嗎？」庫哥白了少年一眼。「不廢話，喏，這平板給你保管。」說完遞給少年超模平板，交代了哪裡開機哪裡充電什麼什麼功能等等。

"Why are you giving me this?" The boy resisted because he felt Data was giving him his last farewell.

"You're looking a gift horse in the mouth? I spliced the mainframe servo-generator to get this voice-enabled super tablet just for you." Data proudly announced.

"So this is it?" The boy had a look of loneliness written all over his face.

Data said, "I'm sorry. I knew that they would track me down sooner or later. Every time I see you since we first met, I have noticed that you have become better and stronger than the time before, just like my program codes have gotten better every time after I tweaked them. It's so inspiring as if I were writing a more powerful computer program. I've been evading the Cloud with all the backdoors and loopholes I know so I can stay and make a better program out of you; no, I meant make a better person."

"Well, then why are you leaving? Where are you going?" Wendi asked. "Didn't you say you have no emotions? Sometimes you actually looked lonely or envious of other people. Those are emotions, aren't they?" The boy unleashed a slew of questions from his chest that he had always wanted to ask Data.

「為什麼要給我這個？」少年有點抗拒他交代遺言式的一大堆說明。

　　「送個大禮給你竟然被嫌棄！這個是我用主程式分出的第二語法驅動的超級平板好嗎！」庫哥一臉驕傲地說。

　　「所以你真的不會再出現了？」少年滿臉的落寞。

　　庫哥歉疚地說：「對不起，其實我一直都知道自己會被追蹤，只是早晚的問題，但和你相處，看你每一次都變得不一樣，更好更強，好像我在重新改寫程式一樣動力十足，特別開心，我就一再想盡辦法打開程式漏洞和你見面，看看你每次還有什麼程式可以被改寫，不是，我是說，有什麼可以幫你的。」

　　「那好好的你幹嘛要走？走去哪裡？」

　　「你不是說你沒有情緒嗎？但我看你有時也會一臉寂寞，或是羨慕別人，那不都是情緒嗎？」少年提出一直以來的疑問。

"There are lots of algorithms in the Cloud, many more than you can ever imagine. The product of these countless algorithmic permutations can manifest as self-propagating algorithms that are like a perpetually self-powered machine. The emotions you saw were the reflection of your emotions which were manifested and matched up with mine out of millions of possibilities by these algorithms. It's like coming up with one solution to a problem even though there are millions of other possible solutions."

"So I'm seeing part of me in you?"

"Yes, we already have a vast amount of data in the Cloud that can self-propagate events billions of years into the future, but in your world, you still have to let each event unfold at its own pace under the laws of physics. While the past programming cannot easily be altered, it is still possible to make different personal choices, kind of like how your soul works."

What Data had just described gave the boy chills. It was as if a conspiracy had been going on all along without his knowledge. "Self-propagating algorithms? Like an oracle who's already known everyone's fate?"

「雲端世界很多運算程式，多到你想不到，後來就在程式與程式之間發展成自主系統控存，你可以說像是不斷電系統，你看到我有情緒是程式運算的結果，是對收到的現實數據做的判讀和反應，很像人類的反應對吧？其實我反應出來的，是程式運算過後對你的反饋，程式運算過程裡，有好幾萬種反饋，而我的主程式和你選擇了其中一種，就好像你遇到一個困難，你的反應和解決方式有成千上萬種，你只選了一種來運用。」

　　「所以有一部份的你，是我的原因？」

　　「對，雲端的世界已經自行運算到好幾億年之後了，但現實世界還是必須按照物理慣性以該有的時間繼續進行。除了物理世界程式沒辦法立即改變外，我們可以左右很多事的發生，就像你們的靈魂一樣。」

　　庫哥這個超乎常理的解說讓少年感覺到害怕，有什麼事情正在看不到的地方祕密進行著。「自行運算？像算命一樣把我們的命運都演算過了一樣嗎？」

"You could say that." Data proceeded to call out a list of future events like an oracle would.

"There are many possible outcomes for the earth's future. This is the reason your people believe in parallel universes, but here's what I can honestly tell you. There can only be one physical world. Your past programming will influence your decisions but there can be only one outcome, which is your current physical world. For example, there is only one Wendi Yu, who can ultimately make only one particular choice, and it will be part of his future. You cannot just delete the decision you made in the past. We are overthinking this. Please just make sure you make the right decisions; otherwise, they will have negative effects on the Cloud, too."

"You've said a lot, but what you're really saying is I am the one who will make the decisions that concern my future?"

"Exactly. You can always consult the tablet because I've already modified it for your physical world. It is no longer connected to the Cloud, so the Cloud and its cloud network regulations cannot mess with the tablet, which you can just use a regular household outlet to charge. My algorithms have already determined that you are quite capable of handling all your problems at hand. It may not make you the master of the

「要這麼說也是可以。」接著庫哥就像抖出什麼天機似的說了一大串有字天書。

　　「地球的未來有好幾種可能的結果發生，所以你們現在才有人相信平行世界的存在一樣，但我可以老實告訴你，物理世界只有一個，程式會誘導你做決定，但真正決定的，還是物理世界，畢竟只有一個游文諦，只會做出一個決定不是嗎？所以你的未來只有一種，你做下選擇的那種，沒辦法砍掉重練哦，想太多了！所以，請你們好好做決定，不然我也會遭決。」

　　「你說那麼多，就是要告訴我，以後我要自己模擬，自己做下每個決定到達未來是嗎？」

　　「說不好的正確。你還是可以用平板的資源，因為我已經把它改成物理世界的能源系統，不能再連上雲端，這樣就不會被雲端協定給封殺。用你家的電就可以充了，我的程式判別出你已有足夠的能力可以解決你目前會面臨的問題，雖然到不了讓你稱霸宇宙的程度啦，但至少可以讓你偶而打贏幾場戰役。」庫哥還是保持著幽默的程式語言。「不是啦，至少讓你在做決定前可以參考一下未來智慧的看法。」

universe, but you'll win a few battles." Data still kept his sense of humor. "Actually, just use it as a reference book before you make decisions."

"Why won't you come back again?" The boy asked again. He was persistent.

"I am part of the programming, too. If I show up here too often, the autobot will detect my activity. I was already pushing my luck as it was, and I almost got caught last time."

"But you said part of you is my reflection. What if I were to use my mind power to call you back? Then you'd have to come back, right?" The boy was becoming stubborn like a willful teenager.

Data smiled. He had a ready answer: "You're smart. You've got potential. You see, my programs are protected from hacking. How do you think I've lasted this long? I am a product of logical algorithms, and my data show that you're not going to run into any troubles now. Even though your mind won't crack my encryption code, the fact is that the human mind has an awesome potential especially during an emergency. Don't underestimate your power. If you know how to use the tablet, you can also harness and control your mind power."

「為什麼你不能再出現？」少年再次問起。

「我也是程式之一，出現太頻繁很容易被程式規約偵測到，這已經是我的極限了，上次我差點沒躲過。」

「可是你說，你有一部份是對應我的結果，那如果我用念力硬是讓你感應到一定要你出現，你也是逃不了的。」少年倔了起來，屬於青少年的任性行為出現了。

不過庫哥反應更是快，笑了笑說：「你真是說不好的聰明，有潛力。程式也是有自我防護措施的，不然我如何生存到現在。我畢竟是理性的運算結果，現在探查你的能力值顯示你已經很難遇到迫切危險了，你這招破不了我設的防禦程式的。其實人的念力在緊急的情況是很強大的，你別小看自己，如果你會運用這平板，你自己就能利用和控制這種念力。」

"So what if you can't come here? I can still talk to you on this tablet," the boy said, still not giving up.

"The Cloud already knew about this backdoor. If they find another breach in the system, for sure they'll know it was me. According to the Master Agreement (cloud network regulations), they can terminate me. Because of this, I've already modified codes in my programs to disconnect me from the tablet. I'm sorry," Data said, trying to sound cool but actually sounding more like he was leaving a will.

"What does it mean to terminate you?" said the boy, looking worriedly at Data as if he were dying.

"No worries. It's not the same as death in humans. It won't hurt." Data was still trying to be funny. "My birth was the product of an aberration in the Cloud, and my appearance here was also the result of a breach in the system, but, unlike those, our encounter had no logical explanations. Maybe it was a matter of probability or what you humans called affinity." What Data had not told the boy was that, as an aberration in the system, he had already outlived most of his peers, who had already been zapped by the system in a matter of days, if not hours.

「你不能出現，那我也可以用這台平板和你溝通啊！」少年仍然不放棄。

　　「因為你這裡的破口已經被發現了，早就記錄在雲端主約中，再用平板連繫我會讓我直接被鎖定，如果被主約協議鎖定，那我就死了！所以我已經寫好程式封鎖平板和我主程式之間的鏈結語言，只能跟你說抱歉了。」庫哥聊起死來雖然也毫不避諱，但聽起來有種斷尾求生的意味。

　　「程式死掉是什麼概念啊？」少年有點擔憂地看著庫哥，彷彿他當場就得死掉一樣。

　　「別怕，和人死掉不一樣，不會痛。」庫哥幽了自己一默，「我的誕生是雲端異變的結果，我的出現也是雲端運算下的漏洞，我們的相識這就沒有規則可循了，就當是或然率吧，不然你就當作是你們講的緣份啦！」庫哥沒有說的是雲端變異的結果可以存活那麼久的只有他這個程式，其他的都很短命，出現運行不到幾天甚至幾小時就被系統吃掉了。

"What is known for certain is that you and I both exist in the same space: Cloud continuum. While we may be invisible to you, you are quite visible to us because every decision you make leaves an imprint in the Cloud. Furthermore, I will never forget you. Just remember that," Data said to the boy. Data was trying to make the boy feel better by not letting him know that the simulated world of the Cloud and the human physical world both share the same risks of human decisions.

"It sounds to me like another fantastical Santa Claus story, except no one's giving any gifts." The boy said, having picked up on Data's sense of humor.

"Ha ha, Wendi, good for you. I see you've really changed. You're gonna to be just fine without me. You're not relying on anyone, and that makes me feel good," Data said to give the boy another dose of positive reinforcement.

At last, it felt like the official good-bye was underway.

"I'm not going to do anything that you told me to. I am never the goody two-shoes kind of guy." The boy was getting antsy.

"Yes, you will because you know I am not coming back, and there'll be no one to fight. You're done." Data laughed.

The boy was defeated. He just wasn't ready. "I'm not really as strong as you think. I…"

「可以確定的是，我存在和你同一空間的雲端，你看不到我，但我可以看到你，因為你做的決定會成為足跡存在雲端中。還有，我不會忘記你的。你只要記住這個就好了。」為了要給少年陪伴的信心，庫哥選擇了不告訴他，自身存在於人類所認為的虛擬世界中和人類活在物理世界裡一樣有風險要承擔。

　　「聽起來就是另一個聖誕老公公的騙局，只是這個真的不會給禮物……」少年也學他幽默以對。

　　「呵呵，形容得還真好。文諦，你已經改變了，沒有我，你一樣會很好，你無須依賴他人，所以我很放心。」庫哥為了再次給少年信心而這麼說。

　　說完，二人正式感覺離別儀式要開始了。

　　「我以後也不會照你的話做，我一直都不是聽話的人。」少年賭氣地說。

　　「你會，因為你知道我不會出現，再唱反調也沒用，你回不去了。」庫哥竟笑著這麼說。

　　少年氣餒，面對庫哥的離開他沒有把握，「我沒有你想的那麼強，我……」

"It wasn't my judgment. Instead, I got it all from the numbers which are never wrong. But the computer cannot predict all the choices you're going to make in the future. Ultimately, the future is in your hands," Data said. "If you run into any difficulties later on, use the tablet first to assess the situation, and then run a simulation."

Before he could finish, the boy became antsy again about Data's instructions. He cut Data off and said, "Well, how about you?"

Data was mildly surprised. "I didn't know you were worried about me."

"You'll have no friend. Then won't you be just like how I was before? What if you need someone to talk to?" The boy asked, not wanting Data to experience what he had gone through in the past without any friends. It was a really bad experience that Wendi did not wish for anyone, especially not the ones he cared about.

"So that's what having a friend feels like. I think I'm starting to get it," Data muttered to himself. "Thank you, Wendi Yu. I'll write a new program to savor this friendship feeling. I'm also going to give it a name. What should it be?" After rolling his eyeballs a few times, Data snapped his fingers and said, "How

「那不是我想的，是數據這麼説，應該沒有誤判的問題。但平板測不出你未來的選擇，所以決定權還是在你。」庫哥回答少年。「如果以後你遇到了説不好的困難，就用平板先分析，或用模擬器……」

　　話還沒説完，少年不耐煩他老是交代後事，出口打斷他：「那你呢？」

　　「你需要擔心我嗎？」庫哥有點意外少年這麼問。

　　「你會沒朋友，不就變成以前的我？下次你需要人和你説話時該怎麼辦？」少年不想要庫哥獨自咀嚼沒朋友的孤獨，他以前的感受太糟，最好不要有第二個人再經歷，特別是自己在意的人。

　　「原來這就是有朋友的感覺，好像有點懂了。」庫哥自言自語，「謝謝你，文諦，我會寫個新的子程式來享受這種朋友感，還要給它取個名字，叫什麼好？」庫哥眼神轉了轉後，彈了個指説：「叫『諦信』好了。如何？」笑笑又挑眉地表示很滿意。

about 'Wendi's Trust'?" He blinked his eyes in delight.

"I feel as if I've accomplished something important, ha ha." The boy had finally come to terms with the fact that Data would be leaving, and there was nothing he could do to change that. Looking at the tablet, he whispered, "You'll always be my hero, Data, until the end of time. No matter what you are or where you are, I'll never forget you." As he looked up, no one was there. Data was gone.

Wendi's eyes reddened as he shouted at the empty field, "Hey, bro! You hear me? Best friends, forever!" He kept shouting to let out his sorrow of losing Data. He kept shouting as if Data would hear him if he raised his voice, even though he knew they were separated by more than just physical distance.

Of course, no one answered Wendi's shouts. The boy stood alone by the riverbank for a very long time. He couldn't move on. This was the first time he had experienced the loss of someone he knew. It felt as if the person had died, and the strong emotions just kept churning inside. It was a good thing there was the familiar soothing sight of sunset, the same sunset Data and he had spent many afternoons under. Soon it was dark, and the boy had to leave.

When it was night, the boy turned on the tablet and saw

「聽起來我變偉大了，哈哈。」少年決定接受離別的事實，知道自己做什麼也改變不了這個結局，於是低頭看著手中的平板，喃喃唸著：「你永遠是我游文諦的兄弟，庫哥，到死都是，不管你是什麼，不管你在哪裡，我不會忘記你。」説著便抬起頭來，但面前一片空曠，庫哥已經消失了。

　　少年漸漸紅了眼眶，對著面前的空曠大喊：「兄弟！有沒有聽到啊？永遠是兄弟啊！」嘶吼著宣示他的義氣與不捨。明知他們的距離不是大聲點就聽得到，少年也只能這樣發洩著，假裝喊得大聲點庫哥就能聽見。

　　當然，也不會有人回答他，少年在河堤邊上站了許久，實在抬不起腳離開，面對自己人生第一個活生生的生離，離的幾乎像死別，少年內心太澎湃了，還好還有夕陽照看著他，那顆和庫哥相處的許多時光中，也一起陪伴他們的夕陽。

　　但過不久少年看著夕陽也回家不再理他了，只好藏起平板轉身踏上黑黑的夜色慢慢地走回家。

a message left for him by Data. It was about setting personal values and goals.

It's night, and all is dark. Ask yourself: Are you getting what you want in life?

Have you ever thought you might be someone different?

Here is a story about someone who changed his destiny:

A man was in the business of selling audio equipment. One day he was at a restaurant when he heard the tapping sound of a cane approaching, and he knew instinctively it was coming from a blind person. The businessman indicated his presence to the blind person, who approached and said, "Sir, I am blind. Could you help?" The blind man took out a wallet and said, "Sir, this brand-new wallet is made of real leather. As you can see, it's soft and nicely polished, and it's only NT$200. Would you like to buy it?" The businessman took out his money right away and said, "I really don't need a wallet, but I am very happy to buy one from you. Here you go, and you can keep the change." The blind man took the money and realized it was a 1,000-dollar bill. He was so happy that he thanked the man profusely. "You have the kindest heart. Thank you so much."

As the businessman was about to leave, the blind man stopped him and said, "Actually, I haven't always been blind.

夜深人靜時，少年打開平板，看到庫哥的訊息——一則關於信念、目標的儲值：

　　夜深人靜，問問自己，今天這個結果是你所想要的嗎？您有想過這輩子還能成為什麼樣的人？

　　來說一個翻轉命運的故事：

　　有一位專門販賣音響器材的企業家，有一天他在餐廳吃飯，聽見後面有手杖敲打地面的聲音，他知道那是一位盲人，於是他用動作，暗示對方。盲人發現前面有人，就停下腳步，上前對他說：「先生，我是個盲人，可否請你幫個忙？」

　　那盲人隨即掏出一個皮夾：「先生，這是全新的真皮皮夾，你一定看得見，這皮柔軟發亮啊！一個只要二百塊錢，請你買我的皮夾吧！」企業家立刻拿出錢說：「我不缺皮夾，但我很願意買你的東西。這錢你不用找了！」盲人摸了一下鈔票，竟然是一張千元大鈔！他不禁心花怒放，連連感謝起企業家：「你是我見過最好心的先生啊！真的很謝謝你啊！」

　　企業家正準備起身離開，盲人又拉住他說：「先生，其實，我並不是生來就瞎眼的，都是二十年前這條街上

It's a big fire at a restaurant on this street 20 years ago." Stunned, the businessman asked, "Did you lose your eyesight in that fire?" "Well, yes. Since then I've been wandering around without a home. The man who caused the fire didn't compensate the victims. I am so unlucky," the blind man said. He was near tears. Patting his shoulder, the businessman said, "Actually, I was injured in that fire and lost my sight, too. The fire also badly disfigured my face. Here, feel it." The blind man was at first overwhelmed then angered by the revelation. He said to the businessman, "That is just totally not fair. You and I were both hurt the same way. Why did you become a rich guy, and I ended up like this?" The businessman smiled and said, "That is a good question. The fact is that I never felt I was unlucky or life was giving me the short end of the stick. When I couldn't see anymore, my hearing became more acute, and I was able to tell very subtle sounds apart. This ability has helped me succeed in the audio business. I believe anything bad in life is a blessing in disguise, and time has proved me right." The businessman never felt that he was a victim, so he was able to adapt and overcome obstacles.

In the end, it is not what happened, but how you react after it happened. Negative thoughts will not bring about positive

餐廳的大火……」企業家愣了一下，問道：「你是在那場大火中受傷失明的嗎？」「對啊！從此我就到處流浪，當年的肇事者也沒賠償，我真命苦啊……」盲人幾乎要流下淚來。企業家拍拍他的肩膀：「不瞞你說，我也是在那場大火中受傷的，我也失明了，還有毀容了……來，你摸摸我的臉，還有傷痕哩！」

這時候，盲人先是錯愕，繼而忿忿不平地說：「老天對我真不公平啊！我們同樣都受傷了，為什麼你可以成為有錢人，而我卻落魄潦倒呢？」

企業家聽了笑笑說：「這個問題很好！其實，受傷當時，我並不覺得我的命運是悲慘的，也不覺得老天對我不公平！因為我失去了視力，所以我有更敏銳的聽力，能夠分辨出音響的好壞；最後，我靠著這一行功成名就。我相信，任何表面的不幸，都是老天要給我更大的祝福。而時間證明了我的信念！」因為他不覺得自己是受傷者，就去修正路線，克服了困難。

結論是，當事情發生時，事件的大小並不重要，重要的是你的想法，念頭負面，命運就無法正面！

changes.

Though perhaps you were not born into the right family and perhaps your road is fraught with more obstacles than other people's, just remember your goal, and give it all you've got.

It is possible to change about 70% of your fate, but it will not just happen. You must face your Achilles heel and stop the negative thoughts that have been tormenting you.

The biggest lie in this world is thinking that you can't. So, let's do this. Find yourself a great goal in life and give it all you've got on achieving it.

Without a doubt, you've got this, Weird, no, Wendi Yu.

The boy chuckled at Data's attempt to cheer him up. He looked forward to a new life.

Every day, he would write a letter to Data with details like when he was thinking about him, what he thought he could do better, how he had used the tablet to solve problems and find more obscure facts, and he even asked him if he should bring a stray dog home. Wendi was trying to pretend that Data was still in his life as a real person and to let Data experience some real benefit of friendship.

In this sense, one could say the boy was the one who had been writing the programs on making friends.

也許您的出身不如別人好，您的遭遇比別人更差，只要知道自己要幹什麼，通過努力，往往可以改變百分之七十的命運；但並非無所事事或做些無謂的事情，而是要直接面對傷痕，終結重覆困擾你的負面思考模式。

　　世界上最大的謊言是，說自己不行，所以，來吧！給自己定一個正向的目標，並朝著那個方向去實現。

　　有問題，你肯定沒問題囉。

　　臨別贈言，庫哥還不忘幽自己一默，少年看罷不禁莞爾，也更期待天明之後的自己與生活。

　　自此以後，少年天天寫一封信給庫哥，說說今天什麼時候想起他、哪些事情他覺得還不夠好、怎麼用平板幫自己解決問題、查到了什麼冷知識，連在路上看見一隻流浪狗想帶回家養也跟他報告，大抵是想假裝庫哥能參與他的人生，希望讓他真正感受到朋友的實惠。

　　這麼說起來，這個充滿朋友感的程式應該算是少年自己寫的。

It is not only the Cloud that is made up of computer programs; our physical world is also made up of discrete and unique programs. Wasn't there a movie that depicted how an innate program regulated how humans conducted among themselves, how the physical world worked, how a tree grew, or even in which direction water flowed?

A life without Data had made the boy more mature. He could now think more independently, and was not affected by his emotions quite as much. He no longer eyed the world with hostility but instead felt closer to people around him. One could say he had been pulled back from the edge of the world. Now, whenever he ran into a problem, he would no longer blame it on other people or his bad luck. Capable of analyzing situations, he was now a tablet himself. He was now able to assess the situation and come up with ways to handle the problem without too much emotion. For problems beyond his capability to solve, he would still consult the tablet for ideas and, in the process of research, come up with more novel ideas of his own. He often found himself not having enough time to do what he wanted to accomplish. The life he had before seemed so pointless and foolish. In comparison, his life now seemed 20,000 times more exciting.

誰説只有雲端世界才充滿程式語言，物理世界裡的
這些不也是一個個的程式語言嗎？人和人相處模式、人
和有形物質的相互對待、樹該怎麼長大、水該往哪裡流，
想想是不是有部電影也這麼説？

　　沒有庫哥的少年變得成熟些，有觀點有想法，也不
再情緒化，不再用防備敵對的眼光看待一切，反而和周
遭的人關係比以往靠近，也算是從邊緣被拉了回來吧。
這時的少年再遇到問題，已經不會先怨對方，怨運氣，
怨天怨地怨黃曆，現在可會分析了，自己就是一部平
板！每次都很有自信能發現問題的根源，不著情緒地給
自己方向和方法，不會的就問平板查資料，在查找資料
過程中又發現新想法，於是又發現自己時間不夠用，然
後再發現原來的自已有多無趣、多蠢，其實可以做的事
很多，有趣的事更多，現在的生活比以往精采了兩萬倍。

The boy has indeed been upgraded to the latest, much-improved version of Wendi Yu. Perhaps at times he still is unsure about how to make friends, perhaps he still does not study as hard as he could, and perhaps habitually he still is overly dependent on his mother, he clearly knows, though, that he can be quite interesting, that he can make friends, that there are people who care about him, and that he is quite talented and capable. When one's inner world changes, one's outer world will change accordingly.

Let's aspire to always remember this truism. Let's make good use of this life for the benefit of all people. Then, we will truly have grown up.

少年的確已經成為全新版的游文諦了，或許還是對交朋友沒特別在行，對課業沒那麼有耐心，對媽媽也還是慣性依賴，不過他至少知道，自己也是有趣的，有朋友的，有人關心的，有能力的。當內在開始進行改變時，外在的世界，也會隨著內在改變。

　　希望這個覺知一直存在，而且善用生命，幫助更多需要的人，這就是長大。

[Epilogue]

Anti-Drug Campaign—A Cautionary Tale

They are not bad kids, just kids who want to hang out with their buddies. Teenagers face issues and interpersonal relationships that have largely extended out of their families and schools. Social structure has undergone rapid changes. Spikes in drug-related crimes are mostly attributable to youths raised in vulnerable and dysfunctional families. However, more and more new drug users are found at schools which brings much anguish to the parents. Government and community leaders have committed immense financial and social resources in their efforts to combat this trend. Fighting drug abuse is no longer just a doctor's job but the responsibility of the whole community.

The focus of prevention should be on the youth who are more susceptible to drug use and addiction. Researchers have found that young people use drugs to relieve their stress and that teachers and counsellors must be skilled in the prevention of drug abuse before they can offer quality measures to identify the most effective ways to mitigate drug use.

Tzu Chi has also poured enormous resources into its anti-drug campaign. In addition to making documentaries as cautionary tales for would-be drug users, Tzu Chi volunteers also seek out educators

反毒——很難從傷害中學習的事

　　孩子不是壞，只是單純喜歡跟朋友在一起。圍繞在青少年身邊的，無非關乎家庭、校園所延伸的人際關係問題。近年來社會結構急遽變遷，青少年學生因吸毒而犯罪的事件層出不窮，除了弱勢家庭與家庭功能失常的孩子之外，校園新興毒品訊息更令父母們恐慌，問題的嚴重，從政府端到民間團體，紛紛投入人力、財力資源，防制毒品問題。讓防毒不再只是警察的工作，需要全民共同攜手，織出綿密的網絡。

　　不忍見青少年年紀輕輕即遭受毒害，一般咸認有必要從青少年階段，積極進行預防與輔導。研究指出，青少年濫用藥物常是一種紓解壓力的方法。而校園教師與相關輔導人員必須有藥物濫用防治的專業，始能提供較高品質之預防與輔導措施。

　　慈濟也為防毒付出極大心力，除了拍攝戲劇，讓更多人理解曾誤入歧途後脫離毒海的翻轉人生經驗，作為警惕之外；更積極培育人才，投入反毒教育宣傳。慈濟人走

and train them to promote the message. Tzu Chi maintains an active presence on school campuses to educate teachers and students on the devastating effects of drugs; they also offer resources for those already addicted so they can quit, saving their families and friends unfathomable agony.

入各校園、社區教育宣導，讓家長與師長們了解毒害症狀與影響吸毒成因，更讓未曾接觸毒品的人，知道毒品的危害；而已深陷毒海的人，更能堅定意志，或尋求協助，終身遠離毒品，不讓自己及親朋好友帶來無限的痛苦。

Here is a brief history of the "Say No To Drugs" campaign spearheaded by Brother Nai-Yu Chen and the teachers and volunteers of the Tzu Chi Teachers Association. It is with great admiration that I share their story with you.

A History of the "Say No To Drugs" Campaign
By Nai-Yu Chen

Illicit drug abuse and addiction has been a social scourge for the last few centuries. Drug-related crimes are continually being reported in the news media on a nearly daily basis. Drug dealers smuggle and sell drugs for profit while addicts steal or commit gruesome acts of violence for their next fix. Flouting traditional social norms and values, girls nicknamed "candy sisters" willingly sell their bodies in exchange for drugs.

Officials from the Ministry of Justice are especially wary that the drugs can hijack the brain into overproducing neurotransmitters. Ultimately, the brain becomes desensitized and would not produce enough of the essential neurotransmitters without the drugs, thereby ensuring the user's dependency on and addiction to them. The 90% relapse and resumption rate is a testament to the power of addiction. Drug addiction problems have become an invisible social menace.

主導接洽反毒活動的陳乃裕師兄與慈濟教師聯誼會無毒有我教育宣導團的老師、師兄、師姊們，他們的團隊長期反毒教育宣傳活動，所累積的心得與分享，著實令人感動。

有毒無我 有我無毒
陳乃裕

「聞毒色變」，是近幾世紀以來人們共同的心聲。透過影音或平面報章媒體所報導之新聞可見，幾乎每日至少有一項社會事件與毒品相關，或是走私販毒；或是吸毒者為了取得購買毒品的經濟來源，販售毒品，逞兇施暴，偷搶他人財物，甚至紅了眼奪人性命，女性吸毒者毒癮上身之際，痛苦難耐，甘做「糖果妹」，以性換藥，價值觀偏頗，道德淪喪。

法務部主管憂心地表示，正因毒品刺激神經傳導物質大量分泌，大腦自動減少該物質分泌，長久下來，體內傳導物質分泌不足，更加依賴外來物質——毒品的刺激，形成不可逆的成癮性，使得這群因毒品而被關入獄中的人，出獄之後，求毒若渴，為此，百分之九十會因毒而再度錯步回籠，他們是社會上看不見的隱形危機。

Many people assume, wrongly, that the drug problems do not concern them personally because they are not addicts, but that is just not true.

Besides the usual at-risk groups, drug abusers can include healthcare workers, military servicemen, and celebrities in the entertainment industry with ages ranging from as young as ten to more than eighty years old. The reasons for their addiction include curiosity, stress, peer pressure, and a lack of knowledge in the substances. But whatever the reason, once hooked, it is often impossible for an addict to quit drugs.

Drug addicts not only wreak havoc on their own families but also harm the society in general because of the hidden social cost. There was a gruesome murder about ten years ago when a paroled drug addict, Yang Zhentang, senselessly clubbed a college professor, Xie Huanru, to death in a riverside park. There was also a girl who was decapitated by a drug abuser, Wang Jingyu, while under the influence of hallucinogens. Countless such gruesome crimes have petrified many in the communities so much that they "Say No To Drugs."

Drugs embolden a person to commit all sorts of crimes. In the Chinese character, "drug" means the ransoming of senses. "Say No To Drugs" needs to be a nationwide movement to bring awareness and an end to drug abuses everywhere.

許多人以為，只要自身不吸毒，這樣的議題應該與己無關，其實不然。

台灣吸毒人口除了社會高關懷成員外，不乏醫界、軍警界、影藝界等知名人士，年齡層從十歲至八十歲均有之。分析其受「毒」荼毒的背景，環境陷阱占多數——好奇、紓壓、透過友人介紹，加上本身對毒品常識不足，輕忽其危害性，往往陷入毒淵而無法自拔。

人一旦染毒，不僅親友是最直接受害者，最終社會大眾也得共同買單。吸毒者為毒犯罪，以及精神恍惚所鑄大錯，從十年前台大副教授謝煥儒在河濱公園突遭剛減刑出獄的煙毒犯楊振堂瘋狂攻擊，傷重不治；至幾年前內湖女童小燈泡命案的主嫌王景玉，被判定是吸食毒品過量導致幻想殺人等；歷年來無辜受害者可謂不可勝數，導致社會人心惶惶。真的說是「有毒無我」啊！

毒品，讓一個人無惡不作，「毒」字，可拆解為毋、主——亦即，毒令人無法做自己的主人！故應理解「有毒無我」的可怖處並反轉之，唯有「無毒有我」——在有我的因緣下，讓社會是一個無毒的天地，才是全民應有的認知與社會責任。

Here is a scene at a typical anti-drug event that Tzu Chi has sponsored.

"Here, grandpa, grandma, come and feel this piece of foil paper. See how it's smooth and shiny? Next…" The volunteer proceeded to roll the paper and press it into a ball. The volunteer then carefully unfolded the ball. The unfolded foil paper now showed wrinkles and holes everywhere. "Drugs leave holes in the brain and make it shrivel, and the brain will never be the same again just like this wrinkled foil paper can never be made smooth again." The audience would gasp, "Oh my goodness!"

Interactive learning like this effectively shortens the distance between the presenter and students, leaving an unforgettable experience, something the traditional didactic teaching method cannot deliver.

"Here's a candy for you," said volunteer presenters as they handed out beautifully wrapped candies to the excited audience. Then, they proceeded to explain that illicit drugs could masquerade as treats for young people such as coffee toffees or gummy bears. "Oh, my…." The audience was aghast and asked the volunteers about the candies that they had just received.

The volunteers assured them that the candies were safe, but they went on to point out a potential scenario on campus: What if drug dealers had handed out drug-laced fake candies at school? They could

在慈濟的反毒教育宣導現場——

「阿公！阿嬤！這是一張錫箔紙，很平整，對不對？接下來……」只見志工們如變魔術般，將完好的錫箔紙瞬間揉皺，甚至捏成一團，待小心翼翼展開，錫箔紙立刻支離破碎：「你們看喔，吸毒會讓大腦破洞萎縮，就像這張揉皺成團的錫箔紙一樣，無法恢復耶！」「這麼恐怖喔！」與會的阿公、阿嬤忍不住咋舌驚嘆。

有別於傳統衛教的專題演講，活動一開始，志工以體驗或闖關遊戲，拉近彼此距離，啟動民眾好奇想了解的興趣。

「這顆糖果請你吃！」「這麼好康啊。」民眾眉開眼笑地接下包裝亮麗的糖果，志工不動聲色繼續介紹毒品種類，看到坊間流通毒品的包裝，竟是咖啡包、小熊軟糖……人人望著手裡的糖果，面面相覷：「這糖果是……」

志工微笑請大家放心，給大家的糖果很安全，但轉而語重心長表示，像這樣的情況時而發生在校園、公眾場所，不肖之人利用人們疏於防備心態，使其接觸毒品，或者給予錯誤訊息：「這不是毒品，是一種提神劑，吃了精神體力變好，就能熬夜讀書，它不會傷害身體的。」讓似懂非懂的青少年誤入毒阱。當下，不少民眾交頭接耳：「這

say to innocent, gullible students, "This isn't a drug. It's an energy booster. Taking it, you'll feel strong; you can stay up all night and study; and it won't hurt you." Then these clueless students became hooked. Upon hearing this, the audience was abuzz with discussion. "Goodness me! I'm going to tell my grandkids about this." "I'm telling my kids to watch out for strangers who give them this stuff." The message was impactful. Drugs are getting too close to home for comfort.

But is merely knowing the horrors of the drugs enough of a deterrent? The presenters followed quietly with a true story.

Over ten years ago, a drug addict, Yang Zhentang, senselessly beat a college professor, Dr. Xie Huanru, to death. All his ribs as well as his skull were broken. Xie's wife, Zhang Meiying, lamented, "How do I hate someone who didn't even know what he was doing?" As a Tzu Chi commissioner, Zhang chose to forgive the perpetrator, but how many other unknown Yang Zhentangs are repeating similar offenses elsewhere in dark corners of society? The audience was silent. There were no easy answers.

Next, they showed a 50-minute documentary, "The Prodigal Son," a story about a drug addict, Huang Ruifang. One day his drug cravings struck. Shivering, he said, "Mom, tie me up, please. Just do it." His mother had no choice but to comply as tears welled up in her eyes. She said, "Ruifang, would you listen to Mom and stop using the drug?"

個，我回去一定要跟阮阿孫講。」「嚇人喔！以後我去接小孩子，一定要特別注意路上陌生人給的東西！」

震撼五分鐘教育，原來毒品與一般大眾如此之近！

知道毒品的可怕，關照家人提高警覺，就能不受毒害了嗎？真實答案，且由真實故事娓娓道來。

志工們緩緩訴說社會上一個個無辜受害者的經歷：「十多年前謝煥儒教授的妻子張美瑛面對丈夫被吸毒者楊振堂打到『十根肋骨全斷，腦殼都破了……』，在最艱難的一刻，她說：『我如何仇恨一個不知道自己做了什麼的人？』身為慈濟委員的她，選擇了原諒，走入人群付出。但，社會上還有多少個楊振堂隱身黑暗角落，反覆上演無辜者的劇碼？」台下一片寂靜，面露無奈。

除了故事講述，活動中也會搭配播映大愛劇場的《逆子》影集，故事主角黃瑞芳，毒癮發作，渾身顫抖地說：「阿母，把我綁起來，拜託妳，把我綁起來……」黃母含淚忍痛綁住了「毒」子：「瑞芳，你甘未能聽阿母的話，賣擱呷毒了？！」但「毒子」終究經不起毒癮的召喚，奮力掙開繩索，悄然離去……

However, his willpower was no match for the call of his drug cravings. Eventually, Huang broke loose and quietly left the house.

After watching it, the elderly folks in the audience were all shaking their heads, "Drugs are just the worst." Some wept quietly as they confided in volunteers, "Actually, our family has one child exactly like that Huang person. Our son is in jail now, and we wish he would just stay there forever. The thought of his release from prison really scares us."

Workshops like this went beyond just teaching people about drugs. They also offered victim families a chance to regroup and heal.

Volunteer presenters said, "Drugs may be scary, but you can just wave your finger and say no. You can also help those already addicted by referring them to the professionals for help. When you do this, you are helping not only yourselves and your families, but the whole society." Everyone nodded their heads in agreement, "Let's all be vigilant about this. Never let drugs sneak into our communities.

"Tzu Chi volunteers visited places from senior centers to indigenous tribes and everywhere in between, talking to people from as young as 10 years old to as old as over 100. Although some of the places they visited did not have audio equipment, blackboards, or even a microphone, the volunteers were always able to make do, come up with substitutes, and deliver interesting presentations all the same. There would be laughter and tears as materials were presented in an interactive and personal

現場長者看了，各個搖頭不已：「毒品實在是害死人！」有些人則低聲啜泣，黯然告訴志工：「其實，這樣的壞囝仔，我們家也有，現在還在監獄裡，我多麼希望他不要出來，一輩子關在那裡！他只要出來，我們都好怕……」

一場場活動，不再只是防毒衛教宣導，更是許多無助家屬心靈療癒的依靠。

志工們殷殷呼喚：「毒品誠然可怕，但只要防患於未然，人人一指頭的力量，拒絕誘惑，勇敢說不，知道有人不幸染毒，勇於舉發，讓專業力量幫助他，也等於幫助自己與家人，還給社會安全有品質的生活。」台下老少頻頻點頭：「這種代誌，咱們真的要很注意，讓毒品進到村里，那可不得了！」

不論是深入長青社區，或是原住民部落，走訪各地區，民眾從不到十歲到一百餘歲均有之，現場宣導環境也往往考驗智慧，有些地方沒有影音，黑板，連麥克風都沒有，但志工們總能臨機變化，以多元素材，在笑中有淚的互動中，唯期盼毒品常識深植腦海，啟發人人對社會的責任感，多一分警覺與關注，少一個家庭愁雲慘霧。

manner. The goal was to get people to understand that drug awareness is everyone's social responsibility. Hopefully, there would be fewer families who are victimized by the drugs.

Substance abuse problems have grown exponentially over the decades, overwhelming the resources of government agencies, law enforcement, and educators. So, what is the best solution? The answer lies in prevention. The best doctor can detect signs of illnesses before they manifest. Prevention and stage-specific treatment for people already in addiction are the ideal solution.

Actually, Tzu Chi volunteers started the anti-drug effort more than 50 years ago by visiting families struggling with drug-related problems. We were able to bring in professionals to help intervene. Our volunteers also spent a great deal of time getting to know the families and to let them know we would care for them in every way possible, and even help them with job training and placement. Those who recovered could turn around and help their old drug buddies who also needed help to kick the habit.

Dharma Master Cheng Yen has said that the true antidote to suffering starts at the beginning. We must do all we can to eradicate drugs from our schools and communities. "Say No To Drugs" is a mission that will go on for as long as there are drug problems. We must keep promoting the anti-drug message and work toward a drug-free society.

數十年來毒品問題甚囂塵上，政府投注大量預算、警力、輔導資源於其上，但總不敵其迅速發展程度！究竟，最好的解決之道在哪裡？或可用未病先防（防微杜漸）與既病防變來概括之。

　　防毒宣教工程，慈濟早於五十年前慈善訪視即開始，對於甫接觸毒品、已吸毒者，交由專業輔導勒戒外，慈濟志工「全人、全程、全隊、全家」的關懷，陪伴當事者與家屬共同面對，沒有時間上限，不僅協助其脫離毒品，還要培養其一技之長，令其走上正途，走回社會，再去勸誡拉拔沉淪的毒友。

　　證嚴法師慈示，若要終結苦難，必須清淨在源頭。只要毒品一天沒有離開社會與家園，「無毒有我教育宣導」的使命就必須持續承擔，讓國人對毒害有共識，起而捍衛無毒家園而共行。

少年與雲端魔法師 The Boy and the Cloud Magican

作　　　者／林幸惠、陳律君
英　　　譯／張恭達（Richard Chang）、Kelly Kuo（本書創意發想）
英譯校訂／湯耀洋（YY Tang）
文字協力／吳琪齡
封底插畫／少年觀護所 小尚
書名頁插畫／林彥睿

發 行 人／王端正
總 編 輯／王志宏
叢書主編／蔡文村
叢書編輯／何祺婷
美術指導／邱宇陞
美術編輯／黃靜薇
出 版 者／經典雜誌
　　　　　財團法人慈濟傳播人文志業基金會
地　　　址／台北市北投區立德路二號
電　　　話／（02）2898-9991
劃撥帳號／19924552
戶　　　名／經典雜誌
製版印刷／禹利電子分色有限公司
經 銷 商／聯合發行股份有限公司
地　　　址／新北市新店區寶橋路 235 巷 6 弄 6 號 2 樓
電　　　話／（02）2917-8022
出版日期／2020 年 8 月初版
　　　　　2020 年 9 月初版二刷
定　　　價／新台幣 300 元

國家圖書館出版品預行編目 (CIP) 資料

少年與雲端魔法師 = The boy and the cloud magician /
林幸惠、陳律君作 . -- 初版
臺北市 : 經典雜誌 , 慈濟傳播人文志業基金會 , 2020.08
面 ；　公分

ISBN 978-986-98968-6-3(平裝)

1. 家庭系統排列 2. 心理諮商 3. 青少年心理 4. 青少年
成長 5. 青少年輔導 6. 青少年問題 7. 親子關係 8. 校
園霸凌

544.67　　　　　　　　　　　　　　　109011569

小樹系列

Little Trees